THE OUTLAW BIKER LEGACY OF VIOLENCE

Outlaw bikers represent a very small percentage of motorcycle riders who join motorcycle clubs, but they receive disproportionate attention due to their mystique, unconventional behavior, and violence. Although the outlaw biker phenomenon started in the United States, it has since spread throughout the world. The involvement of Outlaw Motorcycle Gangs (OMGs) in organized crime at the local, regional, national, and transnational levels fosters violence that puts innocent persons at risk for death or injury and leads to the demonization of "bikers" and the overcriminalization of motorcycle enthusiasts and club members. *The Outlaw Biker Legacy of Violence*, written by internationally known expert Thomas Barker, addresses the legacy of violence in the outlaw biker culture and tackles the implications of the violence that progressed as outlaw biker clubs evolved into adult criminal gangs engaged in crimes for profit over long periods of time and across borders.

Beginning with a history of outlaw bikers and the construction of the "folk devil" of the biker, the book outlines the distinctions between conventional motorcycle clubs, Outlaw Motorcycle Clubs, and Outlaw Motorcycle Gangs, and then traces the expansion of these groups across the globe. This book will be relevant to those interested in the examination or investigation of biker gangs in particular or organized criminal groups in general. It is essential reading for criminal justice students and others studying social groups, gangs, and organizations, or the sociology of deviance, and is also relevant for law enforcement professionals dealing with these organizations.

Thomas Barker, Ph.D., an international expert on Outlaw Motorcycle Gangs, is Emeritus Professor of Criminal Justice of Eastern Kentucky University. A former police officer, police academy instructor, professor at four universities, and Dean of the College of Criminal Justice at Jacksonville State University, Barker has been conducting research and writing on biker gangs for more than 15 years. He is past president of the Academy of Criminal Justice Sciences as well as of the Southern Criminal Justice Association, which annually issues the Tom Barker Award for Undergraduate Student Service in his name. He is the author or coauthor of 17 books and numerous articles, and frequently speaks to groups and in documentaries on organized crime. The Mob Museum, a popular attraction located in Las Vegas, Nevada, presented an Outlaw Motorcycle Gangs exhibit featuring an original video including interviews with Barker.

THE OUTLAW BIKER LEGACY OF VIOLENCE

Thomas Barker

Routledge
Taylor & Francis Group

NEW YORK AND LONDON

First published 2018
by Routledge
711 Third Avenue, New York, NY 10017

and by Routledge
2 Park Square, Milton Park, Abingdon, Oxon, OX14 4RN

Routledge is an imprint of the Taylor & Francis Group, an informa business

Library of Congress Cataloging-in-Publication Data
Names: Barker, Thomas, author.
Title: The outlaw biker legacy of violence / by Thomas Barker.
Description: New York, NY : Routledge, 2018. | Includes bibliographical references and index.
Identifiers: LCCN 2017058153 | ISBN 9781138483897 (hardback) | ISBN 9781138483903 (pbk.) | ISBN 9781351053655 (ebook)
Subjects: LCSH: Motorcycle gangs–United States. | Violent crimes–United States. | Violence–United States.
Classification: LCC HV6439.U5 B3824 2018 | DDC 364.106/60973–dc23
LC record available at https://lccn.loc.gov/2017058153

ISBN: 978-1-138-48389-7 (hbk)
ISBN: 978-1-138-48390-3 (pbk)
ISBN: 978-1-351-05365-5 (ebk)

Typeset in Bembo
by Wearset Ltd, Boldon, Tyne and Wear

This book is dedicated to the memory of our beloved son, Robert Thomas "Bobby" Barker.

CONTENTS

ACKNOWLEDGMENTS

I thank all the unknown persons who helped me in my research into the secret world of outlaw bikers. One of those bikers is Donald Charles Davis, aka The Aging Rebel. His blog and personal help were especially beneficial. The staff at Routledge were their usual kind and gracious selves. Ellen Boyne, my longtime friend, made this task easier to navigate as usual. My wife and best friend, Betsy, provided her usual support and encouragement. I express my gratitude to BSJ who made it all possible.

Thomas Barker

1

THE LEGACY OF VIOLENCE

Introduction

Outlaw bikers represent a small percentage of bikers that join motorcycle clubs—conventional clubs, Outlaw Motorcycle Clubs (OMCs), and Outlaw Motorcycle Gangs (OMGs); but they receive the overwhelming media attention due to their mystique, unconventional behavior, and violence. Outlaw biker violence, especially that which occurs in public settings, puts innocent persons at risk for death or injury, leads to the demonization of "bikers" and the overcriminalization of "all bikers," as evidenced by the police overreaction to the massacre at Waco on May 17, 2015. In effect, the police reaction created a "moral panic," leading to the criminalization of innocent motorcycle riders. However, as with most moral panics, much of this criminalization and labeling is warranted.

Spontaneous impulsive and planned violence, especially that perpetrated by OMCs and OMGs, is a real and perceived danger ubiquitous in outlaw biker culture. Frequent alcohol and other drug use fuels this violence. Physical violence—individual, group, or club-sponsored—is an ever-present predictable pattern of outlaw biker behavior. This is true now and in the past, and likely will be in the future. There is a "legacy of violence" in the outlaw biker culture.

The Outlaw Biker's Legacy of Violence

Pop Culture Response

Spontaneous impulsive and planned violence has been a part of outlaw biker history since the first outlaw clubs formed in the early 1950s. Hunter S. Thompson, in his iconic depiction of the 1960s Hells Angels, wrote, "They inhabit a world in which violence is as common as spilled beer" (quoted in Davis 2015b: 41). Thompson was almost beaten to death by multiple Angels who thought he was taking advantage of them. Outlaw biker legend says the iconic Hells Angels leader, Ralph "Sonny" Barger, saved him.

These deviant—i.e., outside of the social norm—motorcyclists and their individual, group, and club-sponsored violence is a part of contemporary pop culture with TV exposure such as the highly publicized *Sons of Anarchy* (SOA) series and *Gangland* documentaries. These pop culture media portrayed the individual, group, and planned violence of "supposed" outlaw bikers and their clubs, often using known violent criminal men as actors. Several "famous/infamous" Hells Angels Motorcycle Club (HAMC) members with violent criminal histories have appeared on *Sons of Anarchy*. Iconic outlaw leader Sonny Barger, the founder of the Oakland Hells Angels chapter, a former HAMC international president, and best-selling author, has appeared in several SOA episodes. Barger, in spite of his celebrity, is an admitted drug dealer with multiple felony convictions and a history of domestic violence. David Labrava is a member of Oakland HAMC chapter, a published author, and a technical advisor to *Sons of Anarchy*. Labrava's résumé includes multiple felony arrests. Chuck Zito, a frequent SOA actor, is a longtime HAMC member, a bodyguard to the stars, stuntman, bodyguard, boxing trainer, and author. Zito is also an ex-con with a history of impulsive and domestic violence. Rusty Coones has appeared in several SOA episodes. Not listed in his credits is that he is the founder and former president of the Hells Angels Orange County chapter and a two-time ex-con for drug offenses (www.onepercenterbikers.com). There is no listing of the backgrounds of these convicted criminals and violent men in the advertisements for the fictionalized versions of outlaw bikers.

The prolific publication of what some call "crook's books" by outlaw bikers has grown exponentially in the last 10 to 15 years, making celebrities of violent men with unsavory pasts. The book, *Terry the Tramp: The Life and Dangerous Times of a One Percenter* (Ball, 2011), is the story of Terry Orendorff, known as "Terry the Tramp," the longtime leader of the extremely violent Vagos MC. These "crook's books" revel in the real and exaggerated violent nature of the outlaw biker world. Law enforcement officers such as ATF (Bureau of Alcohol, Tobacco, Firearms and Explosives) Special Agents Jay Dobyns (Hells Angels MC) and Billy Queen (Mongols MC) have infiltrated biker clubs and become media celebrities as they recount and embellish the violence they encountered. One paid government informer, Charles Falco, infiltrated the Vagos, Mongols, and Outlaws and wrote several books and appeared in the *Gangland* series.

Academic Response

The popular interest and media attention to Outlaw Motorcycle Gang violence exposed a critical need for scholarly examinations of this deviant and dangerous subculture that was largely ignored by the academic community. This is changing. A limited number of academicians who were former outlaw bikers have published retrospective reinterpretations of their past experiences living in the saloon society of the outlaw biker (e.g., William Dulaney, John Hall, and James Quinn). Limited research studies using secondary data appear in scholarly journals in North America, Australia, and Europe. Outlaw bikers appear as criminal gang topics at professional association conferences such as the Academy of Criminal Justice Sciences and the American Society of Criminology. The "legacy of violence" founding is a part of these scholarly examinations but has not received adequate attention; that is the purpose of this work.

This book documents and supports the growing conclusion that the individual and group violence that has always been present in the outlaw biker lifestyle has increased along with club-sponsored violence as outlaw biker clubs evolved into adult criminal gangs and engaged in crimes for profit over sustained periods of time and crossed borders in searching for crime markets. These adult criminal gangs—Outlaw Motorcycle Gangs (OMGs)—are involved in violent organized crime at the local, regional, national, and transnational levels. Those OMGs engaged in national and transnational drug trafficking have a higher incidence of violence due to the nature of the crime market. Drug sales occur in open-air sites, large sums of money change hands, and sellers have known tendencies for violence (and they are armed) (UNCICP, 2000). The OMGs in the United States and abroad have set up unholy networks of career criminals as they engage in continuing criminal enterprises (CCEs). They use violence as a CCE tool.

The legacy of violence exists in the local, regional, national, and transnational outlaw biker culture. The following inquiry includes well-publicized displays of biker violence. These sensationalized public events shocked not only those in the countries in which they occurred but also citizens around the world. Historically, outlaw biker violence was tolerated and almost ignored, as they kept the violent acts out of public spaces and only killed and maimed each other; however, the incidents explored in this text were in public settings, and some resulted in collateral damage including injuries to and deaths of innocent citizens. The events and criminal actors examined have had a significant impact on the views of biker violence and the preventive actions taken by the state.

This Book's Organization

The background for the *Legacy of Violence* discussion begins with outlaw biker history leading up to the 1969 Altamont Speedway incident and the creation of a new "folk devil": namely, bikers. Then, we present distinctions between types of motorcycle clubs—conventional motorcycle clubs, Outlaw Motorcycle Clubs, and Outlaw Motorcycle Gangs. Next, we trace the expansion of outlaw clubs and gangs throughout the world. Although the outlaw biker phenomenon started in the United States, it has morphed throughout the world. Finally, we present incidents of outlaw biker violence occurring in the United States and overseas as the tendrils of the U.S.-based biker gangs expand transnationally. The expanded worldwide presence of Outlaw Motorcycle Groups as adult criminal gangs ignited club-sponsored violence between competing indigenous and competing U.S.-based biker gangs. Violent outlaw biker events with multiple victims in North America, Australia, Europe, and the rest of the world are data sources for outlaw biker violence.

2

BIKERS AS FOLK DEVILS

Introduction

The number-one controversy surrounding motorcycle clubs is: Are they social *clubs* composed of motorcycle enthusiasts? Or are they adult criminal *gangs*—which would be defined as three or more adult persons who come together to commit crimes for profit on a continuing basis and who happen to ride motorcycles? The answer is yes to the first question—*social clubs*—if the focus is the Thirteen Rebels Motorcycle Club, an American Motorcyclist Association (AMA)-sanctioned motorcycle club composed of law-abiding male and female motorcycle enthusiasts riding all makes and models of motorcycles. The answer to the second question—*adult criminal gangs*—is yes if the focus is the Hells Angels Motorcycle Club (HAMC), a non-AMA-sanctioned motorcycle gang made up of male one-percent outlaw bikers engaged in crimes for profit on a continuing basis. The social clubs and the gang represent extremes on a continuum. However, some motorcycle clubs that do not fit neatly into the club or gang extreme categories can be placed along a heuristic Motorcycle Club Criminal Organization Continuum. This continuum is important because of the consequences of a biased label of all motorcycle clubs as gangs such as occurred following the police and biker shootout in Waco, Texas, on May 17, 2015. As we shall see, the disastrous impact of an overzealous assignment of the gang label to numerous innocent citizens who were guilty only of being in the wrong place at the wrong time points to a premise of labeling theory—labels have consequences (Becker, 1963). The pejorative effects of the "biker" label did not start at Waco in 2015; it has a long history.

Media Biker Coverage and the Creation of a Folk Devil

"Moral panic" and "folk devil" are terms first defined by Stanley Cohen (1972) in his seminal work *Folk Devils and Moral Panics: The Creation of the Mods and Rockers*. Cohen described the media's exaggerated and sensationalized coverage of the Mods and Rockers (British rowdy juveniles identified by their dress). According to Cohen, a moral panic is created when false or exaggerated perceptions of some behavior or groups of persons, particularly minority groups or subcultures, led to the conclusion that the behavior of the group is particularly deviant and poses a threat to society. This is not to say that the behavior of the group or members of the group is not deviant or does not pose a threat, but only that this threat is oversensationalized, often leading to changes in the law and dealing with the group too harshly.

Sensationalized print and nonprint biker coverage began in the summer of 1946 when a dipsomaniac 13 Rebels Motorcycle Club member, Wino Willie Forkner, drove his motorcycle through the wooden fence of a 13 Rebels MC and American Motorcyclist Association (AMA)-sponsored quarter-mile race (Hayes, 2005; Reynolds, 2000). Forkner was thrown out of the 13 Rebels club, and he and other disgruntled and excitement-seeking WWII veterans formed the Boozefighters Motorcycle Club (MC), the first organized Outlaw Motorcycle Club (OMC). The "outlaw" label did not have the connotations it has today; it meant the club was a non-AMA-sanctioned motorcycle club. The Boozefighters MC was one of the several outlaw, non-AMA motorcycle clubs formed by ex-servicemen "letting off steam" and seeking to recreate the companionship and brotherhood experienced during the war (Barker, 2015a; Dulaney, 2005). These early outlaw clubs and the antics of their often-intoxicated members during several exaggerated media events created a new label, *bikers*, that is still a part of popular culture.

The New Folk Devil: Bikers

Sensational and widely published "violent" outlaw biker incidents, such as the Hollister (California) Riot (1947) and the Riverside (California) Riot (1948) created a moral panic. The events aroused social concern over an issue that threatened society. The combination of violent events and sensational public concerns introduced a new "folk devil": outlaw bikers (Barker, 2007, 2015a; McBee, 2015; Reynolds, 2000; Yates, 1999). Following the exaggerated and well-published media accounts, motorcycle club riders, aka bikers, became the number-one enemy of society, requiring more police action, new laws, longer sentences, and increased public hostility and condemnation—that is, they were "folk devils." Exploitative biker movies followed the aroused public interest, adding to the threat posed by "bikers." The first biker movie, *The Wild One* (1953), starring Marlon Brando, became a cult classic and spread the image of the outlaw biker's cultural lifestyle and dress worldwide (Barker, 2007, 2015a; Harris, 1985; Veno, 2003). *The Wild One* was followed by bizarre but popular biker movies such as *Wild Angels* (1966), *Hells Angels on Wheels* (1967), *Hell's Angels '69* (1969), and the enormously successful *Easy Rider* (1969). Many of these movies had actual Hells Angels MC members as actors. These movies built on the interest and lure of the wild biker lifestyle—drinking, brawling, and contempt for mainstream society and its "uptight" morality—and stimulated the growth of Outlaw Motorcycle Clubs throughout the world (Barker, 2015a). British variants of American outlaw biker films were produced in the 1960s and 1970s, stimulating the interest in motorcycle clubs in the United Kingdom (Ward, 2010) as well. Motorcycle clubs or "gangs" became the symbol of hedonistic pleasure and social rebellion and spread globally. The outlaw club the Chosen Few MC of Northern Ireland, founded in the 1970s, followed the dress, rules, membership process, and organizational style known as the Hells Angels Model (Ballard, 1977).

The media attention to the troublesome minority of motorcycle riders in the early development of outlaw bikers created a magnified image of these motorcyclists in the minds of the public

(Austin, Gagné, and Orend, 2010). The sensational media coverage of outlaw biker groups increased as they expanded, nationally and internationally, leading to often-draconian responses by state actors. Historically, the pattern of sensationalized media coverage, political rhetoric, and legislative response to real and perceived biker violence continues today (Morgan, Dagistanli, and Martin, 2010). As can be said of most moral panics, the image of dangerous and violent behavior has a basis in fact. In truth, some, though not all, outlaw bikers are dangerous and violent men, and some Outlaw Motorcycle Clubs are indeed adult criminal gangs (Barker, 2015a).

Outlaw Motorcycle Clubs Evolve and Expand

Motorcycle clubs composed of family-oriented motorcycle riders developed early in the history of motorcycle riding, as soon as motorcycles became affordable recreational transportation. Many of the outlaw clubs examined in this book evolved from fringe members of conventional clubs, as members who were involved in criminal activity or looking for "action" left the family-oriented AMA clubs to join or form outlaw clubs. Some evolved from outlaw clubs into adult criminal gangs, referred to as "Outlaw Motorcycle Gangs" (OMGs) (Barker, 2015a). The archetypal Outlaw Motorcycle Club, the Hells Angels MC (HAMC), founded in 1948 by WWII veterans, evolved into a criminal organization composed of non-veteran thugs and gangsters in the 1960s. The now-criminal gang moved into drug trafficking under the leadership of Ralph "Sonny" Barger and became designated an OMG by law enforcement authorities (Barker, 2015a). Sonny Barger's autobiography refers to the 1970s as the "gangster era" of the HAMC (Barger, Zimmerman, and Zimmerman, 2000). Barger, in spite of his media celebrity, is a convicted felon, ex-con, and admitted drug dealer and cocaine addict. Other U.S.-based outlaw clubs, such as the Outlaws MC, the Pagans MC, the Sons of Silence MC, and the Florida Warlocks MC, followed the HAMC into the evolution of outlaw motorcycle criminal gangs (Barker, 2007). This American expansion is countered by OMCs from other countries moving across national borders. Some expanded into the United States; for example, the Abutres [Vultures] OMC, a one-percent motorcycle club founded in 1989 in São Paulo, Brazil, is the largest Outlaw Motorcycle Club in Brazil and has chapters in Argentina, Japan, Paraguay, Portugal, Spain, and the United States (www.onepercenterbikers.com).

3

MOTORCYCLE CLUBS, OUTLAW MOTORCYCLE CLUBS (OMCs), AND OUTLAW MOTORCYCLE GANGS (OMGs)

Introduction

Defining motorcycle clubs, Outlaw Motorcycle Clubs, and Outlaw Motorcycle Gangs is not an easy task. Most countries outside North America designate motorcycle clubs in three words—Motor Cycle Clubs (MCCs)—and Outlaw Motor Cycle Clubs in four words (OMCCs), and similarly for Outlaw Motor Cycle Gangs (OMCGs). Those in the United States do not divide motorcycle into the two words "motor" and "cycle," so use the following designations: Motorcycle Club (MC), Outlaw Motorcycle Club (OMC), and Outlaw Motorcycle Gang (OMG) or Outlaw Motorcycle Club/Gang (OMC/G).

The distinctions between motorcycle clubs, Outlaw Motorcycle Clubs, and Outlaw Motorcycle Gangs is more than a scholarly debate because of the real social consequences of misclassifications by state actors or failure to take preventive action when such action is warranted (see Box 3.1). Law enforcement authorities as a matter of public policy, must correctly identify which motorcycle clubs are really "clubs" and which are adult criminal "gangs," and act accordingly. This did not happen at Waco, Texas, in 2015, and we will see the disastrous social effects that caused. Legislators must correctly identify and distinguish between clubs as social organizations and gangs as criminal organizations when they pass laws restricting clubs or association or bans on wearing motorcycle-related clothing and symbols.

Laws banning Outlaw Motorcycle Clubs or motorcyclists joining or associating with certain clubs or club members, and the wearing of gang colors, symbols, insignias, and jewelry have been passed at various times in Australia, Canada, Germany, New Zealand, the Netherlands, and the United States. These restrictions on wearing attire and freedom of association demonstrate that labels and labeling have consequences (Barker, 2016).

Perhaps the world's toughest anti-biker law is the Serious and Organized (Control) Act of 2008 of South Australia. This Act allows the South Australian Prime Minister to declare an organization criminal if the members associate for the purpose of organizing, planning, facilitating, or engaging in serious criminal activity (Cash, 2012). Twenty-two bikie [the Australian term for bikers] gangs

---

BOX 3.1 ARREST OF THE "SAINT"

The homeless persons he assists in Texas call 28-year-old Texas biker, Patrick Jim Harris, the "Saint." Harris is a graduate student at Saint Edward's University in Austin. He is an active member of the Grim Guardians Motorcycle Club, whose stated mission is to serve abused and foster children. Patrick's membership in the Grim Guardians and his wearing of the symbols and signs of that membership got him arrested following the Waco Police–Biker shootout in May 2015. Following the deaths of nine bikers, four of whom were shot by the police, the "Saint" was one of the 177 bikers arrested by a knee-jerk overreaction by the law enforcement authorities who arrested everyone they suspected of being a member of an Outlaw Motorcycle Gang. Everyone who was wearing any clothing or patches that signaled membership or association with an Outlaw Motorcycle Club was arrested as being a member of a criminal street gang as defined by Texas statute and held on $1 million bond. Harris is only one of many innocent persons arrested that day.

Source: www.huffingtonpost.com/candy-chand/nightmare-in-waco-bikers-_b_8786502. html. See also The Aging Rebel (February 21, 2017), and Barker, 2016.

---

have been declared criminal organizations, including the U.S.-based Bandidos, Hells Angels, and Mongols. Gang members are prohibited from associating with each other and are barred from entry to designated areas, such as bars and casinos. Anti-association laws such as these rely on police discretion for enforcement and always raise the specter of human/civil rights violations. The Australian law has been criticized for demonizing all bikies and targeting the many to control the few—that is, profiling bikers. A constant complaint among motorcycle riders is that law enforcement authorities illegally profile them for "DWB" (Driving While Biker); that is, anyone on a motorcycle, wearing motorcycle club symbols or insignias, or fitting the stereotypical dress and look of a biker is considered to be trouble and a "likely" perpetrator of criminal conduct.

The American Motorcyclist Association (AMA), the world's largest motorcycle riders' organization, has gone on record condemning motorcyclist profiling:

Motorcyclist Profiling (AMA)
The American Motorcyclist Association has long advocated the rights of motorcyclist and the motorcycling lifestyle. The AMA, in diligently scrutinizing policies directed at motorcyclists, is concerned over motorcycling profiling. This includes motorcycle-only checkpoints and what is a predisposition in many cases of law enforcement officers targeting motorcyclists solely because they are wearing motorcycle-related clothing.

(www.Americanmotorcyclist.com)

In 2011, the state of Washington's Confederation of (motorcycle) Clubs successfully lobbied to get a "profiling of bikers" bill passed in the state legislature. The bill defined profiling as:

RCW 43.101.419
Motorcycle profiling.
(1) The criminal justice training commission shall ensure that issues related to motorcycle profiling are addressed in basic law enforcement training and offered to

(2) Local law enforcement agencies shall add a statement condemning motorcycle profiling to existing policies regarding profiling.

in-service law enforcement officers in conjunction with existing training regarding profiling.

(3) For the purposes of this section, "motorcycle profiling" means the illegal use of the fact that a person rides a motorcycle or wears motorcycle-related paraphernalia as a factor in deciding to stop and question, take enforcement action, arrest, or search a person or vehicle with or without a legal basis under the United States Constitution or Washington state Constitution.

(2011 c 49 §1)

Standing with the governor when she signed the bill banning police officers from profiling motorcycle riders was Robert "Pigpen" Christopher, the president of the Washington Confederation of Clubs and a longtime member of the Outsiders Motorcycle Club. There was irony in that Christopher killed a Portland, Washington, police officer in 1979 during one of the most egregious examples of police abuse of authority against bikers in United States history (Jenkins, April 21, 2011). The Portland police executed a "no-knock" search warrant on the Outsiders MC clubhouse, and Christopher, not knowing who they were, shot the first officer busting through the door. The investigation revealed that the officers obtained the warrant on perjured statements from nonexistent informants and brought with them drugs to plant in the clubhouse. The resulting police corruption scandal led to 58 convictions overturned and 35 pending cases dismissed.

More recently, the Idaho House of Representatives unanimously passed a bill prohibiting motorcyclist profiling and sent it to the Idaho Senate for consideration (Harris, February 28, 2017). The bill would prevent the police from pulling over motorcycle riders or those wearing motorcycle paraphernalia who have not violated any laws.

Law Enforcement Biker Policies

Motorcycle clubs, associations, and interest groups call for law enforcement agencies to formulate, enforce, and evaluate enforcement policies to reduce the errors and unintended consequences of police profiling. That effort begins with the premise that all motorcycle clubs and members are not violent and criminal, but recognizes that all Outlaw Motorcycle Clubs (OMCs) who self-identify or are labeled "OMCs" or "one-percenters" have the potential for spontaneous or planned violence, and some members or cliques of these clubs commit crimes. An even smaller number of Outlaw Motorcycle Clubs are adult criminal gangs—Outlaw Motorcycle Gangs (OMGs)—which are organized for crimes of profit and use extreme violence as a tool in their criminal activities. These unknown numbers of Outlaw Motorcycle Gangs are dangerous and are involved in organized crime at the local, regional, national, and international levels. Outlaw Motorcycle Gangs are adult criminal gangs and their members are on the end of a Criminal Organization Continuum, ranging from clubs to gangs (Barker, 2007, 2015a). Placing the known motorcycle clubs on this continuum is an arduous but necessary task for researchers and policy makers. The data sources available to place any particular motorcycle club on the continuum are often contradictory. There are "official" lists of Outlaw Motorcycle Gangs published by the International Outlaw Motorcycle Gang Investigators Association (IOMGIA), the National Gang Intelligence Center (NGIC), and

the U.S. Department of Justice (DOJ) (Barker, 2015a), but these "official" lists report every identified Outlaw Motorcycle Club as a criminal gang (Barker 2015a). The first attempt to produce a
list by a well-known Outlaw Motorcycle Club member was the 2011 publication, *The One Percenter Encyclopedia: The World of Outlaw Motorcycle Clubs from Abyss Ghosts to Zombies* (Hayes, 2011).
That resource lists 359 OMCs, including many that are classified as criminal gangs by the IOMGIA,
the NGIC, and the DOJ, but Hayes claims they are all clubs and *not* gangs. The 1% Bikers 2015
blog (www.onepercenterbikers.com) lists 105 OMCs and cautions that they are still in the process
of identifying clubs. The author collected newspaper and official documents on OMCs and OMGs
for more than 15 years and divided that information by year and club.

The Criminal Organization Continuum

Gathering data on Outlaw Motorcycle Clubs is difficult because of the variety, size, and "public
face" of the groups. The official sources are overrepresented by the OMCs that receive the most
attention by the media and law enforcement authorities. The groups in Hayes's *Encyclopedia* come
from a knowledgeable biker who is familiar with the outlaw culture, recognizing that OMCs self-
identify as outlaws or one-percenters. The newer 1% Biker blog does not provide the criteria used
for listing. This author's collection of newspaper sources and official documents does not represent
a scientifically accurate sample. The empirically derived Criminal Organization Continuum
developed from the above sources is a heuristic device and uses known indictments, arrests, or
convictions of club members and club leaders for organized criminal activities. The "club" or
"gang" distinction is an empirical question based on the club's, or a chapter of a motorcycle club's,
placement on a Criminal Organization Continuum (Barker, 2007, 2014, 2015a), which is shown
in Table 3.1. The club/gang distinction depends on the extent of the members' organized criminal

TABLE 3.1 Motorcycle Club Criminal Organization Continuum

Club/Gangs	Motorcycle Club	Social Criminal Organization	Outlaw Motorcycle Club (OMC)	Outlaw Motorcycle Gang (OMG)
Basic Structure	AMA-sanctioned or Independent.	In transition (clubs to gangs).	One-percenters (1%).	1% groups—Organized crime entities.
Characteristics	Family-oriented, follow rules of society. Allow male and females to join. Ride all types of motorcycles.	Individuals and small groups commit crime. Members support crime with silence.	Male, primarily white, us-vs.-them mentality, claim territory, fly colors. Individual and clique crimes. Violent or potentially violent. Ride Harley-Davidsons or facsimile.	Majority engage in crimes for profit. Leaders plan and support crime activities. Violence in the extreme. Fight over illicit markets.

Source: Developed by Thomas Barker.

involvement and the club's leaders' involvement in the planning and execution of criminal activities. Further confusing the club/gang distinction is the location of motorcycle clubs within countries and across borders. No single organization defines motorcycle clubs in a country or worldwide to be social clubs or criminal gangs. The members and clubs self-identify as being outlaws or one-percenters, but agree they are not criminal gangs, even though they admit some members commit or have committed criminal acts. However, the available evidence reveals motorcycle clubs vary from social clubs to economic criminal organizations.

Conventional and Social Organization Motorcycle Clubs

Conventional *motorcycle clubs*, which make up the largest number of motorcycle clubs, began to form following the creation of the American Motorcycle Association (AMA)—now the American Motorcyclist Association—in 1924 (Barker, 2007, 2015a). They are, for the most part, voluntary social organizations that represent all races and sexes; have members who ride all makes of motorcycles, foreign and domestic; and behave according to the norms of society. Members join based on a common interest in motorcycles and ride for pleasure and companionship. The first conventional motorcycle clubs sponsored social mixers, charity events, and hill-climbing contests. Their rallies and get-togethers were traditionally family-oriented, and most remain so.

The 13 Rebels MC, a conventional motorcycle club established in 1937, touts itself as a family-oriented motorcycle club adhering to the conventional principles of "No Drugs, No Intimidation, Support Our Military, Support Our Community, Support Our Brotherhood, and Have a Good Time." Their motto, according to their website, is "Not to bully the weak. Not to fear the powerful" (www.13rebelsmc.org). Their Code of Conduct forbids members from selling drugs or committing crimes. Any member convicted of these offenses is expelled from the club. The 13 Rebels MC and other conventional clubs do not claim territory, which is a radical departure from the outlaw clubs. Conventional clubs are careful not to wear the outlaw clubs' three-piece patches, a practice leading to conflict with outlaw bikers. Another conventional club is The Sons of Liberty MC of Texas, which is a tax-exempt, nonprofit corporation not affiliated with or sponsored by any other motorcycle club. This group prides themselves on not being a one-percent outlaw club or a support club of any other motorcycle club. Their mission "is to spread the message of freedom to individuals of all ages from across the world and from all walks of life and economic statuses, how to live philosophically, economically, and practically" (http://solmc.org).

Social criminal organization clubs remain conventional in makeup and outward appearance but have members or small groups of members who engage in largely unorganized and unstructured violence and criminal behavior. These deviant conventional club members may live the biker lifestyle and associate with other deviant bikers in the "saloon society" milieu in which drug-taking, violence, and individual criminal activity are present. These "conventional in name only" bikers drift into criminal activity as the opportunities present themselves, putting them into conflict with other conventional club members. However, the noncriminal conventional member's sense of "biker brotherhood" often creates an unhealthy veil of silence, and their tacit support increases the likelihood that criminal activity in the conventional club will increase (Barker, 2015a). Often, this cognitive dissonance among a majority of members leads a conventional club to evolve into an outlaw club that loses its family orientation, forcing noncriminal, non-supporting members and females out of the "club."

The evolution of groups formed for one purpose—criminal or noncriminal—into adult criminal gangs is not unusual (Barker, 2015b). The Mexican religious drug cartel, La Familia, started out as a vigilante group and evolved into an adult criminal gang (Vergani and Collins, 2015). In their first public appearance in 2006, La Familia members threw five severed heads on a dance floor with the message "La Familia doesn't kill for money, doesn't kill women, and doesn't kill innocent persons. It only kills those who deserve to die" (quoted in Vergani and Collins, 2015: 417). La Familia became heavily engaged in narcotics trafficking. The violent street gang, the Crips, evolved from a 1960s Los Angeles social protest group to become a national crime threat. The Los Angeles Mara Salvatrucha gang (MS 13) began as a self-protection group without criminal purposes to shield immigrants from El Salvador from black and Mexican gangs, and has sometimes been called the "most dangerous gang in the world" after becoming involved in local, regional, national, and transnational organized crime. Even the notorious prison gang, the Aryan Brotherhood, began as a group of California white prisoners protecting themselves from black prisoners. They later became a national criminal organization in prison as well as in the free community. The Phantom's MC in Michigan is an adult criminal gang with many members belonging to the Vice Lords black street gang (U.S. Department of Justice, March 16, 2015). The Dirty Ones MC, a street gang in the Williamsburg neighborhood of Brooklyn, New York, in the 1960s, evolved into an Outlaw Motorcycle Club and then an Outlaw Motorcycle Gang, with chapters in Connecticut, Florida, Massachusetts, Pennsylvania, and Puerto Rico (www.onepercenterbikers.com). The Ching-A-Ling Nomads MC began as a Puerto Rican street gang in the Bronx, New York, before transforming into a multiracial Outlaw Motorcycle Club with chapters in New York, Connecticut, and Virginia. Chuck Zito, who has become a media celebrity as bodyguard to the stars and actor appearing in the TV shows *Oz* and *Sons of Anarchy*, was a member of the Ching-A-Lings MC before becoming a member and founder of the Hells Angels New York Nomads chapter (www.onepercenterbikers.com). The Head Hunters MC, an Outlaw Motorcycle Club in New Zealand, started out in 1967 as a multi-ethnic street gang. Today, they are a serious crime threat involved in drug trafficking and extreme acts of violence.

Other examples of conventional clubs becoming social criminal organization clubs and then evolving into Outlaw Motorcycle Clubs and sometimes adult criminal gangs include the fabled Piss Off Bastards of Bloomington Motorcycle Club (POBOB MC), who are allegedly the forerunner of the HAMC and were a participant in the Hollister Riot. The conventional POBOB club was founded in 1945 as a motorcycle and car club primarily composed of WWII veterans. The car and motorcycle club became an Outlaw Motorcycle Club in the 1950s and is still around today. The Phantom Car Club, founded in the late 1950s in Virginia, transitioned into the Phantom's Motorcycle Club in 1962 and proudly proclaims on their website that they are a 1% Outlaw Motorcycle Club (www.phantomsmc.com). The Sons of Silence MC, started by a U.S. Navy veteran in 1966, appears to have been originally formed as a "drinking club" and then slowly evolved into an Outlaw Motorcycle Club and then into an Outlaw Motorcycle Gang (Barker, 2015a).

Similarly, the Pagans Motorcycle Club, now an extremely violent and organized crime group, began as a benign social drinking group formed by a biochemist at the National Institute of Health. According to a former member who became a journalist and college professor, the group, who rode Triumph motorcycles, became "the baddest of the ass-kicking, beer drinking, hell-raising, gangbanging, grease-covered, roadkill-eating 1960s motorcycle clubs." (Hall, 2008: 7). By the 1970s, the Pagans had become a violent criminal organization under the leadership of John Vernon "Satan" Marron.

The transnational organized crime group the Outlaws Motorcycle Club began in 1935 as the harmless McCook Outlaws Motorcycle Club "out of Matilda's Bar on Route 66 in McCook, Illinois, just out of Chicago" (Barker, 2015b: 207). The original riding social group of young men and women and a number of police officers evolved into a criminal organization in 1969 when the club split into a one-percent outlaw group and a riding group (Lyons, 2003). The Freewheelers MC was founded as a social riding group in Chicago, Illinois, in 1968. The motorcyclists rode all kinds of bikes and accepted a variety of members. A disagreement within the group caused a split, and multiple members joined the Hells Henchmen Motorcycle Club, which was an ally of the Hells Angels (www.onepercenterbikers.com).

Vergani and Collins opine that Australian Outlaw Motorcycle Gangs (they use the term "OMCG") began in the 1960s as "social clubs for men who did not like the typical, quiet family suburban lifestyle" (2015: 417). They were an annoyance to the police, but not a crime threat. However, these Australian clubs became organized crime gangs when the sale and trafficking of drugs became a source of power and wealth. Violence became a norm as these adult criminal gangs jockeyed for dominance over the drug markets. Today, Australian Outlaw Motorcycle Gangs are violent organized crime threats working in combination with Asian and Middle Eastern crime syndicates. A 2014 study in Queensland, Australia, found the common belief that Outlaw Motorcycle Gangs are law-abiding groups "with a few bad apples" was false (Houghton, May 2, 2014). Seventy percent of Queensland "bikies" had serious criminal convictions, ranging from murder to theft, extortion, and drug trafficking. The OMGs with the highest percentage of felons were the Bandidos (72%), Lone Wolf (71%), and the Hells Angels (55%).

In spite of all of this, only a small minority of conventional motorcycle clubs with criminal members actually evolve into Outlaw Motorcycle Clubs or Outlaw Motorcycle Gangs. Typically, the evolution from conventional motorcycle club to Outlaw Motorcycle Club to Outlaw Motorcycle Gang does not occur because the small criminal groups are unable to expand and take control of the leadership positions. In these cases, conventional motorcycle club members who choose not to follow the club's Code of Conduct and become involved in criminal activity end up leaving the club to join outlaw clubs. James Quinn, one of the first former outlaw bikers to get a Ph.D. and move into academia, opined that "bikers, both individually and in local 'chapter' units, often progress, into ever-increasing extremes of deviance over time" (1987: 49). Informal interviews with law enforcement officers and current and former outlaw bikers have confirmed this process. The "in-transit" evolution of social criminal organizations leads to Outlaw Motorcycle Club membership or the formation of Outlaw Motorcycle Gangs.

OMC members reject the norms and mores of society and revel in their sameness—male, majority white, working-class, riding Harley-Davidsons or facsimiles. The outlaw biker club culture is aggressively heterosexual. The men (women are not allowed as members) in these clubs do not fit in mainstream society, exalt in their outlaw status, and defend that status against all challengers (Quinn and Forsyth, 2011). The men live and socialize in a saloon society milieu where all are "slightly criminal" with numerous misdemeanor social disorganization arrests—fighting, drinking, smoking and possession of marijuana, and so on. Road names often describe them or their behavior. In this setting, no one calls them by their "real" names, perhaps because their real names are unknown. They see themselves as outsiders and believe that those who "do not ride" are outsiders not worthy of respect. Even those who do ride are not granted respect unless they are independent outlaw bikers living the "outlaw" code or fellow patchholders. The "patch" on their back makes them different; they are outlaws and proud of it. All Outlaw Motorcycle Clubs have codes of conduct, which include such things as "never steal from another member," "never mess with a member's 'old lady,'" "do not cooperate with the police," "never press charges," "never testify against another outlaw," and the cardinal rule of them all, "never snitch" (Davis, 2015a). It is often said that "snitches are a dying breed," or "snitches get stitches."

OMCs are predominantly white, with many of them excluding blacks from membership consideration in their written rules or constitutions. One example is the Outlaws MC. In 1999, Harry "Taco" Bowman, the International President of the Outlaws MC, after being on the run for two years, was captured, put on trial, and convicted of racketeering, conspiracy to commit murder, and numerous drug and firearms offenses. He was sentenced to life imprisonment. In his appeal, he cited the introduction of the Outlaws' written "whites-only membership policy" as reversible error (*United States* v. *Bowman*, August 20, 2002) because it prejudiced the jury, but the Court disagreed. The Hells Angels MC literally has a written "no niggers" policy in their world rules (Barker, 2015a). Notwithstanding these official policies, clubs that do not allow blacks to join do not have to codify it and risk disclosure in court. As long as one negative vote keeps out prospective members, any racist in the group can keep out "blacks" or any ethnic group member he wishes.

There are, however, some black and multiracial OMCs. The Chosen Few MC was founded in Los Angeles in 1959 as an all-black riding club. Within two years the group took in two white members, making the club one of the first mixed-race outlaw clubs in biker history (www.one-percenterbikers.com). Chosen Few member Cliff Vaughs custom-built the bikes used by Peter Fonda and Dennis Hopper in the 1969 cult classic movie *Easy Rider*. The Sin City Deciples [*sic*] MC, founded in Gary, Indiana, in 1966, began as an all-black motorcycle club but also evolved into a multiracial club. The Sin City Deciples are particularly worrisome to law enforcement authorities because of their recruitment of active-duty military members (Roeder, July 6, 2015). Four active-duty Fort Carson, Colorado, soldiers were charged with the murder of a man outside a Sin City Deciples clubhouse in Colorado Springs in 2012. The Hells Lovers MC, with chapters in Illinois, Colorado, Georgia, Maryland, Michigan, Wisconsin, Texas, and Tennessee, is a multiracial club started by a Mexican American, allegedly because other outlaw clubs disqualified him because of his ethnicity. The Thunderguards MC is an all-black Outlaw Motorcycle Club that was founded in 1965 in Wilmington, Delaware.

By now it should be clear that not all Outlaw Motorcycle Clubs are adult criminal gangs. While most have criminal members, these members are not involved in *club-sponsored* criminal acts with the leaders involved. Some Outlaw Motorcycle Clubs have individuals or small groups involved in criminal activities, but that criminal behavior is not club-sponsored or frequent. Consider, for example, the Brothers Speed MC, an Outlaw Motorcycle Club, founded in 1969 in Boise, Idaho, that has 12 chapters in Idaho, Utah, Montana, and Washington. There is only one documented arrest and conviction of a Brothers Speed MC member for drug trafficking (www.onepercenter-bikers.com). The Free Souls MC, founded in Eugene, Oregon, in 1968, now has chapters in Australia, Europe, and the United States. In that club's history, there are only four documented instances of members involved in organized crime activities (www.onepercenterbikers.com). The Unknown Bikers MC, founded in 1974 in Brooklyn, New York, has expanded transnationally—

to Iceland, Poland, and Puerto Rico—but has not become a serious crime threat anywhere they have gone (www.onepercenterbikers.com). Similarly, the 69ers MC, founded in Brooklyn, New York, in the 1960s, has no documented organized criminal arrests and convictions (www.onepercenterbikers.com).

Without a doubt, many Outlaw Motorcycle Club members lead a deviant, dangerous, and sometimes-criminal lifestyle. Individuals and groups engage in unorganized and unstructured criminal activities. OMC members may engage in spontaneous violent acts or opportunistic criminal acts in addition to the unlawful acts of their deviant lifestyle. Moreover, small cliques in some clubs engage in more organized forms of criminal activity using the OMC's reputation and networks to facilitate their criminal efforts. Their fellow outlaw club members support and condone the organized criminal behavior through their silence and sense of brotherhood, creating a dynamic where association and lack of social control by the peer group enhances the likelihood of criminal behavior. The criminal members of these outlaw clubs use the "power of the patch" to facilitate criminal behavior and intimidate possible victims. Left unattended, they can seize control and cause the clubs to evolve into adult criminal gangs.

Power of the Patch

The majority of Outlaw Motorcycle Clubs identify themselves by a three-piece back patch, which is referred to as their "colors." In most cases, the patch has an arc-shaped top with the club's name, the club logo or insignia in the middle, and a bottom rocker that designates the territory over which the club claims dominance. The Pagans MC is unusual in that it does not have a bottom rocker; this is supposedly to conceal where they are from in order to confuse the authorities. The patch or colors are the outlaw biker's most precious possession. The rank order of possessions is supposed to be colors, then bikes, then dogs, then women. Dogs are useful possessions for security and fighting. Women are useful to sponsor or pressure into prostitution or stripping. Women are seen as subservient and are treated as property, often wearing a "Property" patch, but never a three-piece patch/colors. In the early history of the Hells Angels, women were allowed to be patchholders, but Sonny Barger stopped that practice (Barker, 2015a), as women were not deemed able to prevent the forceful loss of colors.

Colors may not be touched by a non-patchholder without punishment; forgetting to wear colors when required can result in a beating; and losing one's colors for any reason short of death is an unforgivable offense. The patch is a tool of intimidation used against those who travel in the outlaws' world. Ultimately, the "power of the patch" depends on the size and notoriety of the Outlaw Motorcycle Club. Emphasizing the importance of the patch, an Ontario, Canada, Provincial Police Staff Sergeant in charge of a biker enforcement unit, stated, "You can't underestimate the power of the patch. You see someone with the Hells Angels colours, it has to mean something. There is a reputation that patch has built up over the years" (Lejtenyi, October 28, 2016).

In June 2005, a Canadian judge ruled that the Hells Angels Ontario chapter was a criminal group when two members used "the power of the patch" to inspire fear in an extortion victim. The judge ruled that two Hells Angels members "deliberately invoked their membership in the [Hells Angels] with intent to inspire fear in the victim," and they did so by wearing their colors when threatening the victim (Anon. 4, November 17, 2005). OMCs, and especially OMGs, such as the Hells Angels, have a solid violent reputation based on historical incidents that put fear in victims and enemies and discourage witnesses against them.

The three-piece patch displayed on the back of a denim or leather vest is called a "cut." With the exception of Hells Angels members, outlaw bikers typically wear a diamond-shaped 1% patch as well. Legend has it that the 1% designation comes from an early statement from the American Motorcycle Association (now the American Motorcyclist Association), that outlaw clubs represent 1% of the total motorcycle riders. The 1% patch is the mark of the outlaw (Barker, 2007, 2014, 2015a). Outlaws or one-percenters are extremely protective of their patches and very territorially oriented. The majority of OMC violence is related to these two issues—territory and patch.

The Hells Angels were the first to wear a state rocker and claim an entire state (Christie, 2016). The war between competing clubs started immediately thereafter. The Mongols and the HAMC fought for 17 years over the bottom "California" rocker. The Hells Angels said no other club could wear the California rocker, but the bloody war eventually ended with the HAMC declaring that the Mongols had earned the right to wear "California" on their cut (Queen, 2005). The 2002 battle between the Pagans and the Hells Angels in Plainview, New York (to be discussed in more detail in Chapter 7), was an attempt to retrieve Pagan colors surrendered by Pagan members who became Hells Angels (Barker, 2014). See Figure 3.1.

The last grouping of motorcycle clubs on the Criminal Organization Continuum is *Outlaw Motorcycle Gangs*. OMGs are the most deviant and criminal forms of Outlaw Motorcycle Clubs. OMGs are adult criminal gangs organized for crimes for profit on a continuing basis (Barker, 2007, 2015a). These clubs are what Quinn (2001) described as "radical" bikers committed to a criminal

FIGURE 3.1 Outlaw Motorcycle Club Colors.

Source: Photos courtesy of the U.S. Department of Justice.

way of life. U.S. clubs most often labeled Outlaw Motorcycle Gangs are the Hells Angels MC, the Outlaws MC, the Bandidos MC, the Pagans MC, the Sons of Silence (SOS) MC, the Warlocks MC, the Mongols MC, the Vagos MC, and the Wheels of Soul MC (Barker, 2015a). Each of these "clubs" (or chapters of these clubs) have been convicted of being criminal organizations under federal RICO (Racketeer Influenced Corrupt Organization) prosecutions, which provides evidence for the OMG label (Barker, 2015a). While the manufacturing, distribution, and sale of drugs make up the primary activities of these criminal gangs, they are also involved in a wide range of criminal behaviors, including mortgage and insurance fraud and the production of pornography.

Outlaw Motorcycle Gangs sustain a criminal network with the same selection and socialization process that is common for all Outlaw Motorcycle Clubs. Proper, or "righteous," bikers, known to follow the biker lifestyle with reputations for toughness, violence, or criminal behavior are selected to become *hangarounds*, and after club scrutiny for loyalty and commitment, they become *prospects* for membership. Upon successfully completing this phase, they become *full-patched* members. Many prospects, particularly those recruited for selection and membership in OMGs, are bullies with known violent tendencies who single out the weak and gang up on the strong. They may believe five people beating one proves how tough one is, or they may be career criminals who are willing to do any violent act to impress the club's patchholders who vote on their membership. Law enforcement authorities claim that in times of increased tension between OMGs, they tend to recruit violent and criminal members (Dirmann, May 2, 2002). That is a strategy of organized crime groups who have no other option to resolve conflicts among members or with rivals.

Members can and sometimes do leave the outlaw club or gang. Members leave in one of two ways: in either good or bad standing. Those leaving in good standing choose to do so, and the club agrees to it. To leave in bad standing is serious business: the member is kicked out, usually for some violation of trust, such as cooperating with law enforcement or being a snitch. This can result in beatings or even death, depending on the violation. In 2003, a Danish Bandidos member was blown up in his car after being kicked "out bad" (Beckett, September 18, 2003). If the "bad" member is not killed, he gives up all possessions with the club logo, surrenders his motorcycle, and blocks out or removes club tattoos. This author is aware of individuals who had tattoos removed by cutting them off the arms or back, sanding them off with an electric sander, and even one case in which the back patch tattoo was burned off with a butane torch.

This common process of selection, exclusion, and constant social interaction with like-minded peers makes it possible for OMC clubs or chapters/charters to evolve into OMGs, which are criminal organizations in which most (not necessarily all) of the "club" members commit organized crimes for profit with the support or direction of the leaders. The typical OMG organization resembles what is known as the "Hells Angels Model," that is, a strict hierarchical organization—president, vice-president, secretary-treasurer, sergeant at arms, road captain, patchholders, prospects, hangarounds, friends of the club, and associates—with strict control of the organization's members and associates (Barker, 2015a). Outlaw Motorcycle Gangs exist for criminal purposes and control the membership process by selecting and approving only members who have criminal histories, reputations for violence, or a skill needed by the organization (such as having contacts or access to money-laundering opportunities, or being members of legitimate professions such as certified public accountants, lawyers, and the like). The criminal members pay a portion, usually

10%, of all individual criminal proceeds to the club. This is in addition to the often-exorbitant membership dues. This criminal tithing practice is well known and adhered to by all members. Taxing members' illegal activities is a common characteristic of criminal organizations (von Lampe, 2008).

If an OMG member claims not to be a criminal or involved in the gang's criminal activities, his assertion fails because associating with criminals as part of a criminal network is involvement in criminal conspiracy. If the leadership and the majority of the members engage in criminal activities, the "know nothing" defense collapses when supposedly reluctant members show support by acquiescing to members who exhibit violent and illegal behavior.

The presence of club members not directly involved in *organized* crime activities on a continuing basis may represent an attempt by affected club members to argue that a few "bad apples" do not make the club a criminal gang. The limited evidence available strongly suggests that outlaw bikers are involved in serious criminal activities before joining an Outlaw Motorcycle Gang, and their criminal activity increases after joining (Klement, 2016). Furthermore, all members share the same deviant values and socialize and interact with each other on a continuous basis, such as through periodic "church" meetings (a biker term for business meetings) and group "runs." They serve as an important support group for each other. In fact, not attending "church," going on "runs," or supporting fellow patchholders would often be grounds for immediate expulsion from the club. Furthermore, there is little evidence that the club sanctions any of these so-called "bad apples." Criminal offenders are allowed to remain club members unless their crimes embarrass the club, such as child sexual abuse or homosexuality-related offenses.

While OMCs are not necessarily criminal organizations, OMGs are. Whether any particular OMC is a criminal gang is a matter of degree, depending on the numbers of members involved in actual organized crime activities or facilitating these illegal behaviors (i.e., conspiracy) and the nature of the direction and support of the leadership structure. When the majority of members and leaders of an OMC are involved in crime, they are operating as criminal gangs. Even the most crime-oriented and notorious OMGs, however, may have chapters that are free of "organized" criminal behavior (Veno and van den Eynde, 2007). For example, one "classic" Outlaw Motorcycle Club, the Kingsmen MC, founded in 1959 in New York, operates as a criminal organization, but law enforcement officers readily admit that some of the members are not involved in criminal activity (Herbeck, October 8, 2014). Identifying those OMGs that have crime-free chapters is a research project beyond the scope of this work.

Selected Outlaw Motorcycle Clubs Operating as Adult Criminal Gangs

Hells Angels MC

The Hells Angels Motorcycle Club (HAMC) is the model for Outlaw Motorcycle Club organizations. It evolved into a transnational organized crime threat under the leadership of the iconic criminal leader Ralph "Sonny" Barger, who brought together all California HAMCs—both crime-oriented and social-oriented—under his leadership to engage in drug trafficking and other organized crimes (Barker, 2015a, 2015b). Barger also expanded the HAMC outside the continental United States, making the "club" a transnational crime threat.

"Gonzo" journalist Hunter S. Thompson was the first to use the term "Outlaw Motorcycle Gang" in his seminal work on the HAMC—*Hell's Angels* [sic]: *The Strange and Terrible Saga of the Outlaw*

Motorcycle Gangs. In 1994 when all five HAMC Quebec (Canada) chapters voted to go to war with rivals over the Quebec drug market (Cherry, April 16, 2009), it was clear that U.S.-based OMCs were operating as adult criminal gangs (OMGs) in a foreign country. As a result of the vote, a sixth chapter was formed: the elite Nomads chapter, which was composed of the most reputed members of the original five chapters. The Hells Angels had been a crime threat in Quebec, Canada, ever since their arrival in the 1970s, but the vote for the sixth chapter signaled the start of a lengthy conflict between the Quebec Hells Angels together with their support club, the Rockers MC, and the group known as the Alliance, comprised of the Rock Machine MC and a group of drug dealers. The resulting biker war was the deadliest crime war in organized crime history. The ultimate prosecution of the case, known as Operation Springtime, is the focus of a case study by Carlo Morselli (2009).

Operation Springtime

The first Quebec Hells Angels chapter was established in 1977, when it began assimilating or "patching over" existing smaller Canadian Outlaw Motorcycle Club chapters. In 1994, the elite Nomads chapter, which, as has been noted, was made up of the most vicious and criminal Hells Angels members from the other Quebec chapters, began an attempt to control the province's criminal markets—particularly in Montreal, the province's largest city. The Nomads were opposed by a group known as the Alliance, composed of the Rock Machine MC and independent drug dealers, igniting what is known as the Montreal Biker War 1994–2001. This war will be discussed at several points later in this book, but here we discuss the organized crime activities of the motorcycle clubs and the prosecution efforts by Canadian law enforcement authorities.

In the fall of 1999, the accidental killing of a young boy struck by bomb fragments during an assassination attempt led to the creation of Quebec's first specialized organized crime task force— the Montreal Wolverines, composed of the Sûreté de Québec, the Montreal Police, and the Royal Canadian Mounted Police. The target of the Wolverines was the Hells Angels Nomads chapter and the Alliance. The amount of murders committed during the biker war, and the mounting number of innocent deaths, led to the creation of Canada's first anti-gang legislation. The gangsterism legislation, passed in 197, closely mimicked the United States' RICO Act.

The resulting investigations, known as "Operation Springtime," led to the 2001 arrests of 150 bikers and their associates throughout the Quebec Province. Charges included weapons offenses, money laundering, conspiracy, drug trafficking, murder, and "gangsterism." According to Morselli (2009), Operation Springtime, the biggest crime sweep in Canadian history, brought about the following key information:

1   The Nomads chapter of the Hells Angels and its affiliate clubs existed only for criminal purposes (specifically, illegal drug distribution) and recruited only [criminal] offenders.
2   The hierarchy was the governance model within the organization and of any criminal activities that extended from the organization.
3   Climbing the echelons of the hierarchy was the motivational force driving all to participate in criminal activities.
4   Top-ranked members were privileged in that they were able to order lower-level members while remaining active in profitable criminal activities from a distant and secure position (Morselli, 2009: 150).

Other U.S.-Based OMGs

Other U.S.-based Outlaw Motorcycle Clubs have long histories of operating as criminal organizations. The Outlaws MC, under the leadership of the international Outlaws MC president Harry "Taco" Bowman, had a cooperative relationship with the Detroit Mafia (Burnstein, 2016) wherein the two criminal organizations shared gambling operations. At one time the Detroit Mafia put out a contract on Bowman because he was muscling in on the Mafia's craps games. A "sit down" between bosses settled the issue. The Detroit mob, along with safe houses controlled by the Outlaws, shielded Bowman from capture while he was "on the run." Bowman's successor, James "Big Frank" Wheeler, was tried and convicted of similar racketeering charges in 2006 and sentenced to life in prison. Wheeler's successor, Jack "Milwaukee Jack" Rosga, and three other Outlaws MC leaders were convicted in 2010 of participating in a violent criminal organization (U.S. Department of Justice, December 21, 2010). Rosga was convicted of conspiring to engage in racketeering activities as well as conspiring to commit violence in aid of racketeering. The evidence at trial showed that the Outlaws MC, as a criminal organization, planned multiple acts of violence against rival motorcycle gangs, including the HAMC and its support clubs. Rosga was sentenced to 30 years in prison.

The Sons of Silence (SOS) MC, founded in Niwot, Colorado, in 1966 by a former U.S. Navy sailor, evolved into an Outlaw Motorcycle Club and then an Outlaw Motorcycle Gang with chapters in Germany and the United States. Since its founding, the former drinking-and-riding club has been involved in numerous acts of violence and organized criminal behavior. In 1999, two ATF agents infiltrated the SOS MC, and police raided 25 locations in three Colorado cities—Colorado Springs, Commerce City, and Fort Collins. Seized during the raid were 48 weapons, including 24 fully automatic machine guns, four hand grenades, four pipe bombs, and numerous homemade explosive devices (McPhee and Emery, October 9, 1999). The law enforcement authorities arrested 39 SOS members along with the SOS national president. Nearly every member arrested had a felony conviction and could not legally possess a gun. The club's 960-square-foot clubhouse contained a makeshift shrine to Adolf Hitler. The back door to the clubhouse was 1.5-inch steel door, and there were surveillance cameras mounted on the outside of the clubhouse. In spite of a long history of violence and organized crime activities, club spokesmen continue to claim that the club is not an adult criminal gang but just a social motorcycle club with a few members who happen to be criminals.

The Detroit Highwaymen MC, founded in 1954, is Detroit's largest and most violent Outlaw Motorcycle Club/Gang. Their motto is, "Yeah, though we ride the highway in the shadow of death, we fear no evil, as we are the evilest 'Mother Fuckers' on the Highway." Whether this motto is true or hyperbole is not known, but by all accounts, the Highwaymen MC is an Outlaw Motorcycle Gang with chapters in Alabama, Florida, Indiana, Kentucky, Ohio, and Tennessee. Throughout the club's history, members have been involved in organized criminal activities— often, like the Outlaws MC, with ties to the Mafia. In 2007, the FBI arrested 40 members and associates of the Detroit Highwaymen chapter for racketeering charges, murder for hire, cocaine trafficking, vehicle theft, and mortgage and insurance fraud. As a result of this investigation, four police officers were indicted for being members of the Highwaymen or providing information to them and lying to the FBI about their involvement (Anon. 3, March 17, 2008). In 2009, 75 Highwaymen members and associates were indicted for participating in a criminal organization through a pattern of racketeering activity, committing violent crimes in aid of racketeering, and committing federal gun crimes violations (U.S. Department of Justice, May 14, 2009). As of December

2010, at least 10 Highwaymen MC officers had pleaded or were found guilty of racketeering, drug, and weapons charges.

The Avengers MC, another Michigan-based Outlaw Motorcycle Club/Gang, has operated as a criminal organization since its founding in 1967 in Pontiac, Michigan. The national president of the Avengers MC involved the group in a transnational drug trafficking organization (DTO) with a Colombian cartel and "brother-on-brother" murder. The DTO operation began in the 1990s when three career criminals—Brian Chase, Raymond Kelsey, and William Arbelaez—met while serving time in a Minnesota prison (*United States* v. *Ward Wesley Wright*, 2003). Brian Chase was a drug trafficker, as was licensed pilot Raymond Kelsey. Arbelaez was a Colombian national who trafficked cocaine for the Medellin Cartel. This cabal became involved with the Avengers MC when Chase met Ward Wesley Wright, the president of the Avengers MC, when both were bouncers at a Michigan bar. The group formed a transnational drug trafficking organization (DTO). Arbelaez smuggled the drugs from Colombia to Los Angeles, California, where Kelsey flew the drugs to Detroit, Michigan. Chase picked up the drugs in Detroit and delivered them to Wright and Moore, another Avengers MC member. Wright and Moore would then have Avengers members sell the cocaine. A dispute between Chase and Moore over the drug distribution escalated into a murder-for-hire conspiracy where Wright killed his Avengers MC partner and friend for $50,000.

In 1993, Wright and another Avenger member helped Kelsey and Chase steal a United States Forest Service Plane in Atlanta, Georgia. They flew the plane to Colombia to smuggle cocaine back to the United States, and over the next two years, stole two more planes to fly to Colombia for drug payments. In 1996, Kelsey was arrested in Saint Martin (an island in the Caribbean) while flying back to the United States. He agreed to cooperate with the authorities, and the other involved parties were arrested based on his information. Wright was convicted of the use of interstate commerce in the commission of murder for hire, interstate travel in aid of a crime of violence, and conspiracy to possess with intent to distribute cocaine and was sentenced to life in prison.

The extremely violent multiracial Wheels of Soul Motorcycle Club/Gang was founded in Philadelphia, Pennsylvania, in 1967, and is reported to have chapters in 25 states (www.onepercenterbikers.com). Guerilla Docs, a media production company based in the UK, produced a documentary on this Outlaw Motorcycle Club in 2005, and the chief spokesman for the motorcycle club was killed in a drive-by shooting after the filming was over. The Wheels of Soul MC is best described as a criminal organization involved in a number of wars with rival clubs (see Box 3.2).

The Devils Diciples [intentionally misspelled] Outlaw Motorcycle Club/Gang has chapters in Alabama, Arizona, California, Illinois, Indiana, and Ohio. The group has a long history of organized criminal activities. Their most recent racketeering conviction occurred in 2015 when the national president, vice-president, warlord, and three other members were convicted of racketeering and drug trafficking charges (U.S. Department of Justice, February 20, 2015). A federal jury found them guilty of engaging in a RICO crime conspiracy and methamphetamine conspiracy, committing violent crimes in aid of racketeering, and being felons in possession of firearms. Twenty-one other members pleaded guilty to violent crimes. Federal authorities seized 69 firearms and 6,000 rounds of ammunition, and dismantled eight methamphetamine manufacturing laboratories across the country.

Former Mongols MC president Ruben "Doc" Cavazos, at the time of this writing serving a 14-year sentence for racketeering convictions, was a member of the criminal and violent Los Angeles Avenues Hispanic street gang. When he became the National President of the Mongols

---

BOX 3.2 WHEELS OF SOUL MC AS A CRIMINAL ORGANIZATION

In 2011, 22 members and associates of the Wheels of Soul (WOS) MC were indicted by a federal grand jury and charged with being members of a criminal organization engaged in acts of violence, including murder, attempted murder, robbery, assault with a deadly weapon, extortion, and distribution of crack cocaine. The U.S. government alleged that the WOS was the largest mixed-race Outlaw Motorcycle Club in the United States, with more than 400 members in 23 states. The St. Louis WOS chapter was particularly targeted for federal action. This chapter was part of the Mid-West Region of the WOS criminal organization, which included chapters in Indiana, Kentucky, Ohio, Wisconsin, Minnesota, and Illinois. The last two defendants were sentenced in 2013: Anthony Robinson, the WOS regional enforcer, was sentenced to two terms of life imprisonment without the possibility of parole. Jerry L. Peteet, a once well-known criminal defense lawyer, was sentenced to 276 months in prison.

Source: Federal Bureau of Investigation, April 23, 2013.

MC, he recruited Avenues street gang members without motorcycles to join—criminals who were bikers in name only. OMCs who have so-called "bikers" without bikes are in reality criminal organizations at inception and often have ties to other criminal organizations such as the Mafia and street gangs. The Demon Knights MC, founded in New York City, is a support club of the Hells Angels Motorcycle Club and has been involved in criminal activities with the Gambino crime family and the notorious Irish street gang, the Westies (www.onepercenterbikers.com). The Pennsylvania Warlocks MC has ties to the Mafia and came into existence as a criminal organization. The original members had to have committed a theft, murder, or rape to be considered for membership (Barker, 2015a).

The Phantom's [sic] MC of Michigan has members who hold dual membership in the motorcycle gang and the Vice Lords criminal street gang. The Phantom's MC is a black, adult criminal gang with street gang connections acting as an Outlaw Motorcycle Club (see Box 3.3)

BOX 3.3 PHANTOM'S MC AS A CRIMINAL ORGANIZATION

The Phantom's MC has its headquarters in Detroit, Michigan, with chapters throughout Michigan, Ohio, Kentucky, Illinois, New York, New Jersey, Texas, Georgia, and Tennessee. There is also a Nomads chapter that has free rein to roam anywhere at the direction of the president. The so-called "motorcycle club" is heavily involved with the Vice Lords street gang. In 2015, the National President of the Phantom's MC was also the "Three-Star General" over the Vice Lords in Michigan, and numerous officers and members held dual membership in both gangs. The group engaged in murders, shootings robberies, the possession and sale of drugs, and trafficking in stolen vehicles. Members of the Vice Lords assisted them in these criminal activities.

Source: U.S. Department of Justice, March 16, 2015.

Conclusion

Building on the seminal work of Wolf (1991), Quinn opined American outlaw bikers, aka one-percenters, and their motorcycle clubs are not a homogenous group (Quinn, 2001). They are divided into conservative or traditional bikers and radical bikers more inclined to criminal enterprises. The conservative/traditional outlaw bikers come together for the fraternal aspects of belonging to a motorcycle club and engaging in "wild," but not organized criminal, behavior. This type of Outlaw Motorcycle Club is represented by the Rebels MC, which Wolf belonged to and documented. The radical outlaw bikers, although still members of Outlaw Motorcycle Clubs, are more criminally oriented and when present in sufficient numbers can move the Outlaw Motorcycle Club into the Outlaw Motorcycle Gang category. That is what happened to the Rebels MC as they were assimilated—"patched over"—into the Hells Angels MC, an Outlaw Motorcycle Gang. Quinn contends that the Hells Angels, Bandidos, Outlaws, and Pagans are the most "radical" outlaw clubs. While these American outlaw clubs are still considered to be "radical" or adult criminal gangs (Outlaw Motorcycle Gangs), with the transnational expansion of U.S.-based OMCs and the development of large "radical"/criminal OMCs outside the United States, the modern look of OMCs and OMGs has changed dramatically.

The organizations outlined in this chapter are clubs in name only. They are violent criminal organizations, but their violence has become, in most instances, more rational, planned, and lethal because spontaneous violence is "bad for business" (Quinn and Forsyth, 2011). The Hells Angels MC and other U.S.-based biker club/gangs are recognized as dangerous criminal groups in Canada and Australia, and both countries have passed legislation to prosecute them as criminal organizations.

There have been organized biker clubs in Canada since the 1930s, but they did not become a crime problem until the Hells Angels expanded into Canada in 1977. The Hells Angels were not recognized as a serious crime problem until Operation Springtime, and the anti-gang legislation. Canada did not have a legal definition of organized crime until Bill C-95 was passed in the late 1990s defining criminal organizations as:

a   … composed of three or more persons in or outside Canada, and
b   has as one of its main purposes the facilitation or commission of one or more serious offences, that if committed, would likely result in the direct or indirect receipt of a material benefit, including a financial benefit, by the group or by any one of the persons who constitute the group.

The definition excludes gangs of three or more persons that randomly form for the immediate commission of a single offense; Barker (2015b) defined such groups as single-purpose adult criminal gangs. Bill C-95 includes Asian, Eastern European, Italian, and Latin American crime organizations; Outlaw Motorcycle Gangs; and a variety of domestic crime groups (www.rcmp-grc.ca).

In October 2014, the London, Ontario, Licence Appeal Board revoked the "strip club license" of the president of the London Hells Angels by declaring he was the leader of a criminal organization (Richmond, 2014). Official records revealed that the six members of the chapter and three "hangarounds" had 105 criminal convictions between them. The four members of their support club had a total of 25 convictions.

The Australian anti-bikie laws are based on the assumptions that Outlaw Motorcycle Gangs are:

1   composed of criminals and therefore are economic criminal organizations;
2   OMG members associate with each other to conspire to commit criminal acts; and
3   that if the ability of OMG members to associate with one another is circumvented, they will cease to engage in criminal activity (Ayling, 2011, 2011b).

OMC members act with each other and any number of others—support club members, associates, etc.—to commit criminal acts. Whether the third assumption is true or enforceable is subject to debate, and the anti-bikie laws are still being challenged in court and refined. However, this author would add two more assumptions to the list:

1   OMGs have a majority, sometimes not all, involved in organized criminal activities, and
2   OMG officers/leaders are involved in the planning and execution of criminal activities by members and associates.

All this supports that motorcycle clubs can be placed on a *Criminal Organization Continuum*, ranging from clubs to gangs, depending on the number of members involved and the level of support by leaders. The club's criminal history empirically documents its gang status. The Canadian and Australian laws against Outlaw Motorcycle Gangs became necessary because of the transnational movement of OMGs, which is the subject of the next chapter.

4

SPREADING BIKER VIOLENCE

Transnational Expansion of Outlaw Motorcycle Clubs/Gangs

BOX 4.1 OUTLAW BIKER GANG CRIME TRANSNATIONAL TENDRILS

Canada-to-United States Drug Trafficking Organization (DTO)

In 2011, Canadian and U.S. law enforcement authorities disrupted a cross-border drug smuggling operation led by the British Columbia Hells Angels. A Canadian man transported BC Bud—high-octane marijuana grown by the BC Hells Angels—into the United States in hidden containers in 40-foot semi-trailers. He dropped the BC Bud in Seattle and returned to Canada with cocaine. Eight members of the DTO were convicted. The driver received 12 years in prison (U.S. Immigration and Customs Enforcement, May 6, 2013).

Malaysia, Singapore, and Australia DTO

In 2014, an international operation by the Royal Malaysian Police, the Singapore Central Narcotics Bureau, and the Australian Federal Police smashed a methamphetamine DTO. Two Australian Outlaw Motorcycle Gangs, the Rebels and the Finks, led the operation (D'Cruz, November 7, 2014).

Australia-to-Thailand DTO

Anthony Bagnato and Wayne Schneider were partners in an Australian fitness center. Bagnato was Schneider's bodyguard. Both men were also Australian Hells Angels members as well as drug dealers and traffickers. The men traveled to the notorious sex-tourism resort of Pattaya, Thailand, about 90 miles south of Bangkok, to set up a drug smuggling operation between Thailand and Australia. In December 2015, Schneider was abducted and kidnapped by five men outside a Pattaya luxury villa he shared with Amad "Jay" Malkhoun, the former president of the Australian Comancheros MC, another notorious transnational OMG. Malkhoun, following the typical OMC/OMG omertà, said he did not hear a thing and that he slept through the abduction and kidnapping. The next day Schneider's naked, badly beaten body was found in a shallow grave; Schneider had suffered a broken back. Bagnato fled to Cambodia, where he was arrested and returned to Thailand for trial. In February 2017, Bagnato was found guilty of the murder based on testimony from his accomplices. He was sentenced to death by the Thailand court (www.bangkokpost.com).

France-to-Belgium DTO

Two Belgium Hells Angels on a bus to Belgium stopped at a customs checkpoint near Paris, and 25–34 kilograms of marijuana were found in their suitcases. Their excuse was that they were in financial difficulties, forcing them to act as drug mules for the Hells Angels. The unsympathetic French court sentenced them to 30 months in prison, fined them 88,690 euros, and prohibited them from entering French territory for three years (Anon. 5, February 17, 2017).

FIGURE 4.1 Outlaws in Germany.

Source: Photo courtesy of the U.S. Department of Justice.

Introduction

The examples demonstrate the increasing tendrils of Outlaw Motorcycle Gangs as they spread their crime and violence globally. The Hells Angels Motorcycle Club—an Outlaw Motorcycle Gang on the Criminal Organization Continuum—paraphrasing the British Empire saying, proudly proclaims, "The sun never sets on the Hells Angels." With chapters in all continents except Antarctica, the U.S.-based OMG is correct. Other OMC/OMGs in the United States and other countries have followed the HAMC lead. The social network of OMGs is worldwide and growing. This expansion translates into global opportunities for criminal enterprises—that is, organized crime—to be planned, coordinated, and facilitated by Outlaw Motorcycle Clubs/Gangs in one country and committed by Outlaw Motorcycle Clubs/Gangs in another country—that is, transnational organized crime. The effects of criminal enterprises are felt across borders, and the underlying motive is personal gain. Albanese opines "Transnational organized crime (TOC) can be considered the modern extension of organized crime in the globalized era" (Albanese, 2012: 3). That Outlaw Motorcycle Gangs are heavily involved in transnational organized crime is a point emphasized by the United Nations.

The United Nations Centre for International Crime Prevention (UNCICP, 2000) described Outlaw Motorcycle Gangs as a hierarchical criminal group, with relatively strict lines of command from the center:

> there is a degree of autonomy present in regional organizations under control of the group.… In some cases, regional hierarchies appear to operate a 'franchise model' in which regional groups pay money and give allegiance to use the name of the well known criminal group, helping to improve their influence and instill fear into their competitors.
>
> *(UNCICP, 2000: 77; see Box 4.2)*

The United Nations (UN, September 2002) provided a description of OMC/G activity in Australia. They noted the following features:

- There is a series of criminal groups that operate mainly on the East Coast of Australia. They have a rigid hierarchical structure. The basic element of the structure is the Chapter, headed by an Executive, which operates in a specific area. The Executive is composed of an elected president, a vice-president, a sergeant at arms, a secretary/treasurer, and a road captain. The president has absolute control over the Chapter. There are several categories of hierarchically ordered groups termed "prospects," "associates," and "hangers-on." Most are governed by a set of rules known as a "constitution" or "by-laws," and some have written codes of ethics.

BOX 4.2 OMG REGIONAL HIERARCHY

According to the United Nations,

> Outlaw Motorcycle Gangs have a defined hierarchal structure [the Hells Angels Model], divided into sub-groups [chapters or charters] each operating in specific geographic regions. The basic element of the structure is the chapter, which operates in a local area and governed by a president. This individual has absolute power regarding decision-making and rules with dictatorial power. Each chapter has a degree of independence from the others. Drawn largely from the white working class, outlaw motorcycle gangs have a strong social identity. Gangs are entirely male. While membership has been traditionally granted after a strictly internal process (including a period of probation), such procedures have weakened in some areas in an attempt to acquire more members. The most highly organized gangs have also targeted prospective members who have particular skills (such as lawyers, accountants, realtors, or chemists). Most outlaw motorcycle clubs are governed by rules known as "by-laws," or a constitution.… Violence is also often key to their activities.
>
> *(UNCICP, 2000: 77)*

- They are involved primarily in drug production and distribution (mainly of amphetamines and cannabis) as well as in prostitution and trafficking of stolen vehicles. Activities cover a range of crime types, including trafficking in counterfeit goods, fraud, insurance scams, money laundering, armed robbery, illegal immigration, organized prostitution, extortion, manufacturing of firearms/ammunition, trafficking in explosives, trafficking in endangered species, murder, assault, arson, tax evasion, social security and licensing fraud, and illegal fishing.
- There is extensive use of violence among the groups as well as a high level of penetration into the legitimate economy.
- They cooperate with other organized criminal groups abroad.
- There is no indication that OMCGs have any influence on the political process.
- Members are drawn from the same social background, that is, white, male, and working-class communities. Only males are granted membership status, but women are associated with the gangs, serving as prostitutes, drug couriers, or intelligence gatherers.
- Members are largely Australian nationals, but come from a variety of ethnic origins (though Asians are excluded from membership).
- There is a cluster of approximately 30 different gangs with a total number of 3,000–5,000 full members and approximately 7,000 associate members.

Perhaps most important to this treatment of the biker legacy of violence is the UN's contention that individual gangs traditionally use violence toward other clubs and individuals as well as within the gangs themselves. Competition between clubs has led to territorial wars. The UN reported 10 publicized murders of members by rival gangs between 1997 and 2001. They note,

> The threat of violence is widespread and is essential to ensure group cohesion. The sergeant-at-arms is responsible for internal discipline and punishment.
>
> The gangs have strongly penetrated the legitimate economy in Australia, owning and operating restaurants, hotels and security companies. Also gangs are active in the construction and adult entertainment industries and have made some investments in both property and the stock market. Similar gangs are also present in the United States, Canada, Norway, Denmark, Finland, Netherlands, Austria, Sweden and New Zealand. Some cooperation between OMCGs in different countries occurs.
>
> *(UN, September, 2002: 93)*

American OMGs Move First

The transnational expansion of Outlaw Motorcycle Clubs/Gangs across state borders and continents was in the past largely a phenomenon of U.S.-based clubs, such as the Hells Angels, Outlaws, Bandidos, and a few lesser-known OMGS expanding into Australia, Canada, and Europe. The availability of criminal markets where the perceived risks were low and profits were high was recognized by the Hells Angels in the 1960s and soon spread to other U.S.-based OMCs. These adult criminal gangs extended their criminal networks into potential criminal markets, most notably drug trafficking. The social networks common among OMCs and OMGs can supply or facilitate the production, distribution, and sales of a wide range of illicit goods and services—producers, transporters, sellers, and buyers.

The global extension of OMCs and OMGs has changed in the last decade. Today, a wide range of Outlaw Motorcycle Clubs/Gangs (OMC/Gs) from various countries are crossing borders for access to criminal markets. They generally have the same goals—profit and power. This movement of OMC/Gs throughout the world spread the "legacy of violence" common to outlaw biker culture. Violence is the only contract enforcement device open to OMCs acting as adult criminal gangs.

At the time of the initial expansion of U.S.-based clubs outside the continental United States, there were indigenous OMC/Gs in countries targeted for expansion. Many of these homegrown gangs were already in the organized crime business and resisted, often violently, the encroachment of the U.S.-based outlaw bikers. They were unwilling to give up their autonomy and crime markets to the American interlopers. In return, some indigenous OMC/Gs responded to the interlopers by moving across their national borders and "setting up shop" on U.S. soil or in other countries and competing in the same crime markets. This back-and-forth transnational movement has spread the crime networks and violence traditionally associated with outlaw bikers globally. The natural animosity that exists among OMCs ensures that violent clashes among rivals will occur as they jockey for respect and territory. This book traces the cross-border expansion and later provides selected examples of the violence that has accompanied the transnational movement.

Transnational Expansion of North American Outlaw Motorcycle Clubs

United States

U.S. OMC/Gs, such as the Hells Angels MC, the Bandidos MC, the Outlaws MC, the Mongols MC, the Warlocks MC, the Sons of Silence MC, and the Vagos MC, have expanded internationally—41 different countries as reported in 2012—where they fight with each other and indigenous OMC/Gs over territory and crime markets (Barker, 2014, 2015a). Reliable statistics on these secret deviant groups are hard to come by. Some OMC/G s provide listings of their chapters on websites or on Facebook, but these are often not accurate and timely. Researchers know this, but use them as the best source available.

The largest OMC/G in the world is the Hells Angels Motorcycle Club (HAMC), which has charters (chapters) on every continent except Antarctica. Their official website lists charters in the United States, Argentina, Australia, Austria, Belgium, Bohemia, Bulgaria, Brazil, Bosnia and Herzegovina, Canada, Caribbean, Chile, Croatia, Cyprus, Denmark, Dominican Republic, England, Ecuador, Estonia, Finland, Germany, Greece, Holland, Hungary, Iceland, Ireland, Italy, Japan, Latvia, Liechtenstein, Lithuania, Luxembourg, New Zealand, Norway, Northern Ireland, Malta, Peru, Portugal, Poland, Romania, Russia, Serbia, Slovenia, Slovakia, South Africa, Spain, Switzerland, Sweden, Thailand, Turkey, Ukraine, Uruguay, and Wales (http://hells-angels.com/world/).

OMC/Gs rely on a network of puppet or support clubs to support their recruitment efforts. These support clubs facilitate the gang's criminal networks and act as surrogates in wars with rivals. The largest Hells Angels support club is the International Red Devils MC, which was founded in Sweden in 2001. In 2015, a now-defunct website reported that the Red Devils MC had chapters throughout the world: Australia, Belgium, Brazil, Bosnia and Herzegovina, Chile, China, England,

Germany, Italy, Luxembourg, New Zealand, Singapore, South Africa, Sweden, Turkey, and the United States.

The Hells Angels are not without competition from other expanding U.S.-based OMC/Gs. As of November 2016, the Bandidos MC listed chapters in the United States, Australia, Belgium, Brazil, Costa Rica, Denmark, England, Estonia, France, Finland, Germany, Greece, Holland, Indonesia, Ireland, Italy, Malaysia, Panama, Paraguay, Russia, Serbia, Singapore, Spain, Sweden, Thailand, and Ukraine (http://bandidosmc.com). The Outlaws MC, the traditional enemy of the Hells Angels and ally of the Bandidos, has matched the HAMC expansion. The Outlaws have chapters in Australia, Belgium, Canada, Czech Republic, England, France, Germany, Hong Kong, Iceland, Ireland, Italy, Japan, Jersey (Channel Islands), Montenegro, New Zealand, Norway, Philippines, Poland, Spain, Sweden, Switzerland, Thailand, and the United States (www.outlawsmcworld.com). The Sons of Silence MC, which was originally formed in Colorado, has 30 U.S. chapters and five chapters in Germany (U.S. Department of Justice, May 8, 2015). The Mongols MC, known to be extremely violent, is one of the latest U.S.-based outlaw biker clubs to expand transnationally. Their official website lists chapters in Australia, Mexico, and Thailand, with plans to move into Canada (http://mongolsmc.com). The 1%er Bikers website report greater expansion, listing Mongols chapters in Australia, Belgium, Brazil, Canada, England, France, Germany, Indonesia, Israel, Italy, Malaysia, Mexico, Singapore, Sweden, Switzerland, Thailand, and the United States (www.onepercenterbikers.com), but there is no way to check the accuracy of this claim. The Mongols Webmaster did not respond to inquiries, claiming that the reason is "because that is club business." We do know that in 2013, the vast majority of the Australian Finks MC patched over to the Mongols.

The U.S.-based Vagos MC, aka known as the Green Nation because of the Mexican heritage of the original founders, was founded in San Bernardino, California in 1967. Biker legend maintains that the original members, because of their Mexican heritage, were denied membership in the other biker clubs, including the Hells Angels MC. In recent years, the Vagos MC, known to be extremely violent and criminal, expanded internationally and has chapters in Australia, Brazil, Germany, Mexico, Sweden, Switzerland, United Kingdom, and the United States. The Vagos MC website lists chapters in Australia, Brazil, Canada, England, Germany, Mexico, Scandinavia, and Switzerland (http://vagosmcworld.com). This expansion has resulted in violent clashes with other U.S.-based and indigenous Outlaw Motorcycle Gangs, increasing the "legacy of violence" this book highlights.

There are two Warlocks MCs calling themselves Outlaw Motorcycle Clubs. One is the racist Pennsylvania-based Warlocks, who publish on their website "ALL WHITE! RED AND WHITE" (Barker, 2015a). This group came into being as a criminal gang, requiring members to commit or have committed a serious felony (Barker, 2015a). They have been a serious crime problem in the Delaware Valley of the United States since the 1970s but appear to have no international chapters. Another is the Florida-based Warlocks MC, which, according to their official website, was founded aboard the USS *Shangri-La* during the Vietnam War in 1966 (Barker, 2015a). The website list 38 chapters—31 in the United States and seven in Canada, England, and Germany.

An enigma in the study of OMC/Gs is the Iron Order MC, founded in Jeffersonville, Indiana, in 2004, which is one of the fastest-growing motorcycle clubs in the United States. The Iron Order MC claims not to be an Outlaw Motorcycle Club (OMC) because they have a large proportion of members who work in the criminal justice system, including police and corrections, and in the military. However, their pugnacious violent conduct, such as picking fights with other motorcycle clubs and shooting their way out, belies their statements. They may not have evolved into an adult criminal gang, involved in crimes of profit (yet), but the group is mimicking the violent behavior of OMC/Gs and is spreading that violence transnationally. The Iron Order MC has established chapters in Aruba, Bonaire, Brazil, Canada, Curacao, England, France, Germany, Puerto Rico, Slovakia, and South Korea (www.onepercenterbikers.com). If the club does not rein in the violent behavior of its members, it will likely transition into an OMG and become a problem wherever they expand. The other Outlaw Motorcycle Clubs will treat them just like any other outlaw club—Give No Respect; Get No Respect.

There are smaller U.S.-based Outlaw Motorcycle Clubs that have expanded overseas, sometimes with the support of larger clubs such as the Hells Angels or the Bandidos. The Satans Soldiers MC, which is aligned with the Hells Angels MC, was founded in Bronx, New York, in 1968. They have at least two chapters in Australia and have had violent conflicts with Bandidos in both countries. Surrogate warfare is not uncommon among Outlaw Motorcycle Clubs. The Chieftains MC is an Outlaw Motorcycle Club that was founded in Lawrence, Massachusetts, in 1976, and expanded to Denmark in 1977. They now have or have had chapters in Denmark, Netherlands, Norway, and the United States (www.onepercenterbikers.com). The small Banshees MC, founded in New Orleans in 1966, established a chapter in Germany in 1989. In the 1980s the Banshees' U.S. chapters carried on a shooting war with the Texas Bandidos.

Canada

Outlaw Motorcycle Gangs are defined in Canada by the Royal Canadian Mounted Police (RCMP) as,

> any group of motorcyclists enthusiasts who have voluntarily made a commitment to band together and to abide by their organization's rules enforced by violence, who engage in activities that bring them and their club into repeated and serious conflict with society and the law.
>
> *(Katz, 2001: 231)*

According to Katz, they are considered to be the most serious crime threat to the country, in effect "the enemy within" (Katz, 2011). The pernicious threat the Hells Angels represent to the Canadian criminal justice system was made clear by the arrest and conviction of the law enforcement officer considered to be Quebec's leading biker expert, Benoit Roberge. Roberge was convicted of passing information to the Hells Angels on three separate drug investigations (Cherry, March 16, 2017). For $125,000 he sold out his police agency and received an eight-year prison sentence, not to mention the damage he did to his reputation and social standing.

The U.S.-based Hells Angels are considered the major organized crime problem of Ontario, Canada (Anon. 1, 2002). There were 14 HAMC chapters in Ontario in 2002; 83 percent of the known members had criminal records, and 53 percent had records involving drugs, violence, and weapons. There are approximately 450 full-patched HAMC members in Canada, and that number does not include the puppet and support gangs that do much of the "dirty work" of the HAMC, insulating the patched members from prosecution. Gangsters Inc. reports that a resurgence of the indigenous Rock Machine MC, decimated during the Montreal Biker War (1994–2002) between the Hells Angels and the Rock Machine, has reemerged, leading Canadian authorities to believe that another biker war is coming (http://gangstersinc.ning.com/).

The Bacchus OMC/G is reported to be the largest Outlaw Motorcycle Club in Canada (www.onepercenterbikers.com). This club was founded in 1972 in New Brunswick, and its size and reputation for violence have allowed it to remain an independent club without any control efforts by other clubs. Bacchus has chapters in New Brunswick, Nova Scotia, Newfoundland, Prince Edward Island, and Ontario, and all of the Bacchus chapters are known as violent criminal organizations.

The Canadian Loners MC, founded in 1979, has an erratic history, with members leaving to join other indigenous motorcycle clubs such as the Satan's Choice MC, Para Dice Riders, the Rebels, and U.S.-based clubs such as the Bandidos and Outlaws. It is reported that there are Canadian Loners MC chapters in Canada, England, Germany, Italy, and Spain (www.onepercenterbikers.com).

The Canadian Rock Machine MC has a bizarre violent and criminal history. Founded in 1982 by a former member of the white supremacist "SS" motorcycle club, the "club" became involved in crime and controversy. This group did not wear colors or leather cuts, purportedly to hide their identity from the police. Many (perhaps the majority) of the members did not own or ride motorcycles, making them another example of a "motorcycle club that wasn't." They were a group of criminals involved in drug trafficking. As alluded to earlier, the Canadian Rock Machine MC was the major antagonist against the Hells Angels in the Montreal Biker War, the bloodiest organized crime war in history. The biker war that took place between 1994 and 2002 was fought over drug marketing in Montreal and other areas of the Province of Quebec (Barker, 2015a). In 2001, the war appeared to be over when the warring clubs and their lawyers met in a Quebec City courthouse and declared a truce. The truce lasted for two months, and then the Rock Machine MC became a probationary Bandidos MC affiliate. As the Bandidos and the Hells Angels are bitter enemies, the war resumed. The original Rock Machine MC dissolved sometime around 2006, but it reappeared in 2007 and has now expanded into Australia, Canada, France, Germany, Great Britain, New Zealand, South Africa, Sweden, Thailand, and the United States (www.onepercenterbikers.com). According to the RCMP, the Rock Machine MC still operates as a criminal gang in the Canadian province of Manitoba, where they are engaged in drug and firearms trafficking. The 2012 RCMP *Operation Dilemma* against the Rock Machine MC in the Winnipeg area seized firearms, ammunition, pipe bombs, and other commercial explosives, along with cocaine, methamphetamine, and marijuana (RCMP, 2012/2013).

Mexico

The Solo Angeles MC was founded in Tijuana, Mexico, in 1959. Although they do not have chapters outside Mexico, they have close ties to the Hells Angels MC, and there have been attempts to establish ties in the United States with HAMC approval.

OMC/Gs' Transnational Expansion in Europe

In October 2015, the Netherlands, Germany, and Belgium signed an agreement for a closer partnership with each other against Outlaw Motorcycle Gangs—both U.S.-based and indigenous—

that have become a major crime problem (Kidd, October 10, 2015). These "criminals without borders" have become an international phenomenon, leading to attention and action by governments, the United Nations, Europol, and INTERPOL (Barker 2014; Barker 2015a). There is a sordid history behind the 2015 action taken by the agreement between these three bordering countries. In 2010, Europol warned that the Hells Angels Motorcycle Club was expanding into Eastern Europe with chapters in Bulgaria, Croatia, Czech Republic, Greece, Hungary, Poland, and Turkey (Europol, 2010). Eastern Europe and the Balkans are vital to drug smuggling routes from Central and Southeast Asia, where most of Europe's heroin and marijuana originate. The HAMC was using the "Balkan route" from Turkey to engage in drug trafficking. Although other U.S.-based OMGs were also making this move, the HAMC, as the largest and most criminal and violent OMG in the world, has received the most attention.

Law enforcement authorities are aware that violence in the extreme tends to follow any HAMC movement. Europol warned that the extreme forms of violence used by the HAMC and other OMC/Gs included the indiscriminate use of firearms and explosive devices, such as grenades, in public spaces. Furthermore, Europol warned in 2012 that the expansion of both U.S.-based OMC/Gs and other countries' OMC/Gs into Europe had increased the number of OMC/Gs to 700 different chapters (Europol, December 21, 2012). This expansion came from Australia (Comanchero MC and Rebels MC), Canada (Rock Machine MC), and the United States (Mongols and Vagos). The cross-border expansion of local European groups such as the Satudarah Maluku MC and the Blue Angels MC from northwest Europe added to the increased numbers of OMC/Gs throughout Europe. Europol prophetically stated that the expansion will lead to violence as the new gangs encroach on the territory and crime markets of already established motorcycle gangs. Particularly disturbing was the trend of these OMC/Gs to recruit street criminals, far-right militants, football hooligans, and ex-military men who do not even have motorcycles, driver's licenses, or a commitment to the "biker" lifestyle—that is, "bikers" without bikes (Rossington, January 7, 2013).

In 2013, a major international operation was investigated by authorities in Spain, Germany, Luxembourg, Netherlands, and Austria, with the cooperation of Europol, Eurojust, and Spanish Guardia Civil and National Police. Authorities executed 32 house searches and arrested 25 Hells Angels MC members on the Spanish island of Mallorca (Europol, July 24, 2013). The recently founded HAMC Mallorca chapter opened with the support and protection of Hells Angels in Germany and Luxembourg. European indigenous OMC/Gs outside the United States followed the lead of the U.S.-based groups, and crime markets and violence expanded internationally.

International Expansion of Selected Indigenous (Non-U.S.-Based) Outlaw Motorcycle Clubs/Gangs

Australia

By all accounts, the five largest OMCs in Australia are the U.S.-based Hells Angels and Bandidos and the indigenous Comanchero, Lone Wolf, and Rebels MCs. The Comanchero and Rebels, along with other Australian OMCs, have expanded transnationally.

The Australian Comanchero MC first expanded to Bosnia, and then to Spain (McNab, 2013). The Rebels MC, which is the largest biker club in Australia, was established in Brisbane in 1969 as the Confederates, with a Confederate flag as their logo. They changed the name to the Rebels and kept the Confederate flag. They now have chapters in Thailand, Indonesia, and Singapore, and their website lists chapters in the United Kingdom, Costa Rica, the United States, Sweden, and Fiji (McNab, 2013). In 2015, the Australian Rebels established three transnational chapters (Humphreys, 2015). They have been involved in wars with the Bandidos and the Hells Angels, including armed battles in public places—pub parking lots and airports. The movement of Australian OMGs into southeast Asia prompted the Australian gang task force to sponsor a Southeast Asian conference attended by 75 state and territory police forces from Australia, Thailand, Malaysia, Vietnam, Singapore, and the United States (Groom, October 7, 2014).

The Australian Coffin Cheaters MC, founded in 1971, has three chapters in Norway. The Australian Gypsy Jokers have affiliated with the U.S. Gypsy Jokers (Barker, 2015a), and in addition have established chapters in Germany, Norway, and South Africa.

The Notorious MC, founded in Australia in 2007, is another example of "an outlaw motorcycle club that wasn't" (Barker, 2015a). The members of this "motorcycle club" were recruited primarily from Lebanese and Pacific Islander street gangs. Their dress consisted of Nike Air Max shoes, designer tee shirts, and styled hair—not the typical biker outfit (www.onepercenterbikers. com). The derogatory term "Nike Bikies" was applied to this group because of their dress and the fact they do not ride motorcycles. This vicious street gang was dismantled and declared no longer active by the New South Wales police in 2012.

There are other OMC/Gs that are street gang criminals without motorcycles. Recently, a Comanchero MC member who was facing deportation to the United Kingdom said in his defense that he was not a bikie and could not ride a motorcycle (Mann, February 28, 2017).

Denmark

Outlaw biker gangs—particularly the HAMC, the Bandidos MC, and the No Name MC (NNMC)—are a major problem for the Danish National Police (Klement, 2016). The NNMC began in Denmark in 1972 and has since spread to Finland, Poland, and Sweden (www.nonamemc.dk/history.htm). In 2007, the HAMC created a puppet support club, called AK81, which was composed of mostly street gang members who did not own or ride motorcycles (Klement, 2016). Many AK81 members and other support club members morphed into the Devils Choice MC, which was founded in Denmark in 2010 as a Hells Angels support club (www.onepercenterbikers.com). The AK81 patch is red and white with a devil's head, similar to the famed HAMC "death's head." This group has expanded to Iceland, Norway, Spain, and Sweden.

The United Kingdom

There are numerous OMCs with the name Satans Slaves MC, including one founded in Shipley, England, in 1967. This biker club now has chapters in England, Scotland, and Germany. A violent encounter between this group and their English rival, the Road Rats MC, will be discussed in Chapter 7.

Germany

The Gremium MC, founded in 1972, is reported to be the largest Outlaw Motorcycle Club in Germany, with 155 chapters worldwide: more than 70 chapters in Germany as well as chapters in Austria, Belgium, Bosnia and Herzegovina, Chile, Denmark, Germany, Italy, Isle of Seven (Fuerteventura), Macedonia, Norway, Poland, Serbia, Slovenia, Spain, Thailand, Turkey, and Venezuela. In 1988, the outlaw club was declared a criminal organization by the Minister of Baden-Wurttemberg. That label was removed after the court ruled in 1992 that it could not prove whether the criminal acts were not just the actions of individuals in the club—a constant problem in the prosecution of Outlaw Motorcycle Clubs (www.onepercenterbikers.com). The Gremium MC and the Hells Angels MC are in constant conflict. Two chapters of the Frankfurt Hells Angels were banned from the city in 2011 and their assets seized because of their history of weapons and violence (Amoruso, November 1, 2011).

The Black Pistons MC, the largest support club of the U.S.-based Outlaws MC, was founded in Germany in 2002. The first chapter in the United States was established, also in 2002, when the Ohio-based Satan's Syndicate MC patched over to the Black Pistons. The following year the UK Birmingham Chapter of the Brotherhood MC patched over to the Black Pistons MC. The Black Pistons MC has a network of Outlaw MC support chapters in Australia, Belgium, Canada, England, Germany, Iceland, Norway, Poland, Scotland, Switzerland, the United States, and Wales (www.onepercenterbikers.com).

The Netherlands

OMCs have been in the Netherlands since 1970, but they were not recognized as a serious crime threat until the late 1990s, when it became known that the Amsterdam Hells Angels were involved in a transnational drug-trafficking network. The Dutch government has tried and failed to ban the Dutch Hells Angels as a criminal organization four times, at the time of this writing. Other Dutch OMCs have joined the HAMC as serious crime and social order threats. In 2013, there were 12 OMCs reported to be in the Netherlands; the "big five" OMC/Gs, based on their number of chapters, are Satudarah MC (indigenous), Hells Angels MC (U.S.-based), No Surrender MC (indigenous), Trailer Trash MC (indigenous), and Red Devils MC (an HAMC puppet club) (Blokland, Soudijn, and van der Leest, 2017). The No Surrender MC made news in 2014 when three members fought with the Kurds in Iraq fighting against ISIS (Amoruso, October 11, 2014).

The Bandidos and the Mongols have also recently established chapters in the Netherlands. The Bandidos chapter was formed by a former member of the Hells Angels Nomads chapter in Oirsbeek (Amoruso, March 20, 2014). The Hells Angels chapter disbanded when members of the chapter killed the chapter's president and three other officers. They remained silent and were acquitted.

Immigrants from the former Dutch colony of Moluccas established the Satudarah—"One Blood"—MC in 1990. The group's bottom rocker is Maluku, now part of Indonesia. The logo of the club is a double warrior head—one white and one black—to represent the multicultural nature of the club. The Satudarah was banned in Germany for being a threat to social order after multiple drug and weapons offenses and violent clashes with the Hells Angels MC. The Satudarah has chapters in Australia, Belgium, Canada, Norway, Singapore, Spain, Suriname, Sweden, Switzerland,

Thailand, and Turkey (www.onepercenterbikers.com). They are in constant tension with the Hells Angels as they move into territory claimed by the HAMC (Barker, 2015a). The Dutch No Surrender MC, established in 2003 by a former Satudarah president, has 26 chapters in the Netherlands as well as chapters in Belgium, Denmark, Germany, and the United States (Blokland, Soudijn, and van der Leest, 2017).

New Zealand

OMC/Gs, particularly the Hells Angels MC and several indigenous groups, have existed in New Zealand since the 1960s. Except for the U.S.-based HAMC, the New Zealand clubs were not an organized crime threat until the 1990s (Gilbert, 2017). The Highway 61 MC, founded in Auckland, New Zealand, in 1968, has chapters in Australia and New Zealand, and is a violent organized crime threat in both countries. In the late 1990s, the Highway 61 MC moved into the trafficking of marijuana. Other clubs followed their lead, but the Highway 61 MC is the only New Zealand MC known to have expanded outside the country. One particularly infamous Highway 61 MC member, Malcolm Rewa, will be discussed in Chapter 6.

Poland

There are numerous OMCs that call themselves Road Runners MC. The Polish Road Runners MC was established in the Silesia region of Poland in 1978 (www.onepercenterbikers.com), and was reportedly the first outlaw biker club in Poland. In 2006, the Road Runners MC established their first chapter in the United States with members of Polish heritage in Chicago, Illinois. They now have chapters in Austria, Belgium, Poland, and the United States. To date, they do not appear to be much of a crime problem in the countries where they have chapters.

Russia

The Night Wolves MC is a curious Outlaw Motorcycle Club that is hard to classify. The club was founded in the 1980s in the Moscow area, originally as a group organizing illegal rock musical concerts because of the Soviet Union's music ban. The group later self-identified as an Outlaw Motorcycle Club and is considered to be a group of "social activists" because of their close ties to Russian President Vladimir Putin (www.onepercenterbikers.com). They have chapters in Bulgaria, Latvia, Macedonia, Romania, Russia, Serbia, and the Ukraine. They have used force, including murder, to prevent other Russian bikers and clubs from joining U.S.-based OMCs (www.onepercenterbikers.com).

Thailand

A new motorcycle club, Crims MC, has appeared on Facebook and biker sites in recent years. This motorcycle club is based in Thailand and claims to have chapters in the Channel Islands, Corsica, England, France, Norway, Scotland, the United States, and recently established chapters in Australia (www.goldcoastbulletin.com.au). They may be a Bandidos support club, but this has not been verified.

Conclusion

The transnational expansion of OMC/Gs has exponentially increased the global nature of outlaw biker crime and the accompanying extreme violence that will be covered in the next chapter. The cross-border expansion began with U.S.-based OMC/Gs but expanded to groups from all over the world. This author once said in jest that "OMG" actually means, "Oh My God, they are everywhere." Unfortunately, there is a lot of truth in that statement. OMC/Gs are indeed just about everywhere, and their crimes and violence have followed their transnational expansion.

The transnational OMC/Gs show support for one another in world runs and attendance at funerals and important trials. In 2008, at a trial in South Dakota for two Hells Angels members shooting at a group of Outlaws MC members attending the Sturgis bike rally, the first five rows on the defense side were filled with Hells Angels members from California, British Columbia, and Luxembourg (Verges and Martin, November 16, 2008). The trial surrounded the first violence at Sturgis between rival biker gangs since 1990, when a Sons of Silence member shot an Outlaws member in a bar fight in which a Sons of Silence member was stabbed. The façade of brother supporting brother can mask problems among the clubs.

The international expansion of U.S.-based OMC/Gs is not without its problems for the former autonomous U.S. clubs. According to Jay Dobyns, an ATF agent who infiltrated the Arizona Hells Angels, the European Hells Angels outnumber the voting American Hells Angels at their world meetings, often creating delays in "patching in" full members and other decisions (Dobyns, 2009). This has created tension between the U.S. Hells Angels and the European Hells Angels, with some HAMC members complaining that the "tail is wagging the dog."

The tension between the Hells Angels international clubs pales in comparison to what happened within the Bandidos MC following what is referred to as the Shedden, Ontario, Massacre. On Sunday, April 8, 2006, Canadian police were called to a rural farmhouse in Shedden, Ontario, by farm owners who made a frightening discovery. They found a minivan and a tow truck with a car attached to it. Inside the vehicles were the bodies of eight men. The investigation revealed this massacre was the worst mass murder in Ontario's history. Court testimony revealed the murders were the result of an "internal cleansing" of errant Bandidos members ordered by the International President of the Bandidos MC in Texas. It is considered the largest biker murder incident in world history (Barker, 2015a).

The victims turned out to be six full-patched Bandidos members, one prospect member, and a Bandidos associate. All were connected with the No Surrender Crew of the Toronto Bandidos, who were named after a branch of the Irish Republican Army (IRA). Among the deceased bikers was John "Boxer" Muscedere, the national president of the Bandidos MC, Canada. According to testimony from an informant (a patched member of the Winnipeg Bandidos who dealt drugs and did not ride a motorcycle), the Texas Bandidos ordered the murders because the "motorcycle club that wasn't" was not paying their dues or following Bandidos rules. The alleged rules violations included not getting permission and approval before giving Bandidos membership and giving membership to individuals who did not own or ride motorcycles. According to the informant, the eight slain bikers were killed during a "patch-pulling" ceremony by the probationary Winnipeg Bandidos chapter. The Winnipeg chapter would be given full status after the "patch pulling" (Barker, 2015a). The assailants were reportedly under the influence of methamphetamine, so even if murder was not the original intent, the results were disastrous.

Six Bandidos were arrested and charged with the murders: Wayne Kellestine, a traitor from the Toronto chapter; Michael Sandham, the president of the Winnipeg Bandidos chapter and a former police officer (a stigma in outlaw biker culture); and four other members of the Winnipeg Bandidos chapter. Following the so-called "patch-pulling ceremony," the Texas Bandidos learned that Kellestine and Sandham were not eligible for Bandidos membership because Kellestine did not own a motorcycle and Sandham was a former police officer. The Texas Bandidos also learned that the Winnipeg Bandidos chapter had several members who did not ride or own motorcycles. The Winnipeg Bandidos chapter's membership was revoked, and they were barred from wearing Bandidos colors (Appleby, June 22, 2006).

While there are no more Bandidos in Canada, the fallout for the Bandidos OMC/G was not over. At the time this activity was taking place between the Canadian Bandidos and the Texas Bandidos, there was a move by the Australian Bandidos to unite with the European and Asian Bandidos to support the resurgence of the remaining Canadian Bandidos (McNab, 2013). The International Bandidos President in Texas, Jeff Pike, objected and ordered the Australians to "stand down" and follow orders. They did not, which created bad blood between the Texas and Australian chapters. Australia has the highest per capita outlaw club membership in the world, and the Australian Bandidos have chafed at the autocratic leadership of Pike for some time (McNab, 2013; as well as formal and informal interviews with present and former Bandidos).

There was also trouble brewing in Europe among the Bandidos chapters. Pike and other U.S. Bandidos were worried about the Australian and European Bandidos approving membership for Middle Eastern prospects and members without bikes. The global rift led to the creation of two distinct Bandidos clubs: the North American Bandidos versus the rest of the world. On July 17, the following message appeared on the Bandidos official website, "Though we share a common name and a similar patch, we are no longer associated with the Bandidos MC in Europe, Asia and Australia" (www.bandidosmcunitedstates.com). The Bandidos of the continents of Australia, Asia, and Europe now have their own national chapter presidents.

All the Bandidos chapters worldwide are listed on the official website; however; in 2011, Pike—who was no longer the international president, but the national North American Bandidos president—made subtle changes to the logo, making it an obese Mexican man wielding a machete and a pistol. The Bandidos have two different logos depicting the so-called "Fat Mexican," one for the North American Bandidos and the original for the Bandidos from the rest of the world. The Bandidos racketeering indictments following the 2015 shootout at Waco, Texas, will likely drive a further wedge between the two Bandidos factions.

5

THE CULTURE OF VIOLENCE IN THE OUTLAW BIKER COMMUNITY

Introduction

Australian outlaw biker expert Arthur Veno opines, "Violence is central to club life. It is implicit in the rules, the way members live, and their interactions with other clubs" (Veno, 2009: 139). As pointed out in the last chapter, outlaw biker violence is a worldwide phenomenon; therefore, we examine it from a global perspective. We start from and build on what is considered a comprehensive definition of outlaw biker violence described by Quinn and Koch (2003). They identified two categories of OMC violence:

1   *Spontaneous expressive acts*, which usually involve one or a few members in violent crimes directed at rivals or other actors from within the saloon society milieu (e.g., bar fights).
2   *Planned expressive acts*, which are directed at rival groups and are either planned by established cliques or chapter/regional/national officers or tacitly reflect the priorities off the chapter or club.

See Box 5.1.

Quinn and Forsyth (2009) attribute the term "saloon society" to Hunter S. Thompson (1966) and his groundbreaking examination of the Hells Angels. The term "saloon society" refers to the "taverns and nightclubs of urban centers and the roadhouses on their outskirts" (p. 256). These bars, taverns, and roadhouses are well known to motorcycle riders. One can go to the Internet and search for biker bars and find a list in any area nationwide. Bikers know where to find them; they are safe areas for those who want to be the "top dog" in the social setting.

Spontaneous Expressive Acts

The definition of *spontaneous expressive [violent] acts* includes collateral damage—injury and deaths—occurring to citizens, or those who come into contact with a "bad" outlaw biker acting out of

---

BOX 5.1 JACK ROSGA—OUTLAWS MC LEADER

"Jack Rosga led an outlaw motorcycle gang that was violent at its core," said U.S. Attorney MacBride of the Eastern District of Virginia.

> As the gang's national president, Mr. Rosga declared war on the rival Hell's Angels and ordered violent acts on rival gang members. Mr. Rosga admitted to undercover federal agents that he expected to go to jail for leading this violent motorcycle gang, and the jury convicted him of conspiracy to commit racketeering and violent acts. He spent decades dedicated to a criminal way of life, and he'll now spend decades in prison paying for those crimes."

(Anon. 6, April 9, 2011)

Rosga was convicted of conspiring to engage in racketeering activities and conspiring to commit violence in aid of racketeering. He was sentenced to 20 years.

---

impulsive or irrational motives fueled by alcohol or other drugs. This happens both inside and outside of the saloon society milieu.

Random Violence

Quinn and Koch (2003) as well as Barker (2007, 2015a) contend that impulsive, often irrational, violent behavior is a constant possibility in the lawless saloon society frequented by outlaw bikers. Innocent, clueless citizens are often the victims of this violence because they are not aware of the saloon society "rules" to be followed when encountering an outlaw biker (see next section). Civil society exists when lawful or social rules are adhered to, but that is not true for outlaw bikers. Citizens do not expect to be punched out when accidentally brushing up against another person in crowded space, but that happens when the other person is an outlaw biker, especially when the outlaw biker is a "prospect," seeking membership, and under observation by his peers to see if he has "class."

Outlaw bikers have a known low threshold for violent reactions to any slight or signs of disrespect (Barker, 2015a). Exemplifying this reality is an incident in which a California man, coming out of a bathroom in a blues lounge, accidently bumped into a member of the Sundowners MC. After the mishap, several bikers dragged the man out to the parking lot and beat him severely. Dazed after the assault, he made it to his van and left, almost hitting a motorcycle with his vehicle. Bikers then pursued him in a wild ride on the street before they cornered him. One came at him with an iron pipe, and another attempted to bust out his window with a flashlight. The frightened man sped off, running over and killing one of his tormentors. The driver turned himself in later, and after an investigation, was not charged in the death of the biker. The ruling was that it was self-defense (Gettleman, March 1, 2000). This man's name was kept out of the media reports to prevent retaliation. In another incident, a Canadian casino patron was badly beaten because he accidentally knocked over an outlaw biker's stack of chips (Bolan, March 16, 2007).

Davis (2015a) reported the case of a Colorado man driving with his girlfriend and three-year-old son who "cut in" on a pack of Valiants MC members. One of the outlaw gang members pointed a gun at the man, forcing the man to pull over. He was severely beaten, his headlights smashed, and his tires slashed. Cutting in on a pack of outlaw bikers on a run is considered to be disrespectful. The average citizen does not know that outlaw bikers make their own rules.

Disrespect extends to those who, for whatever reason, claim to be a member of an Outlaw Motorcycle Club—a mortal sin to outlaw bikers. One drunken German teenage tourist to Australia suffered internal bleeding between his skull and the lining of his brain, as well as a broken leg and lacerations to his scalp and face from a baseball bat beating by a Hells Angels member. He had been caught claiming to be a member of the Hells Angels (Butcher, November 14, 2014). Similarly, a young British man who thought it would enhance his status among women got a Death's Head [Hells Angels logo] tattoo, suffered for his action (this is surprising because most tattoo parlors will not tattoo an outlaw logo on a nonmember). Several Hells Angels members caught him, and they took the tattoo off with a metal grinder (Whittingham, August 19, 2015).

In the early 2000s, Anthony Benesh, a volatile and often irrational construction worker in his forties and longtime resident of Austin, Texas, decided he wanted to start a Hells Angels chapter (Smith, May 19, 2006). Benesh announced his intention to family and friends and put it out on social media. He had no known affiliations with the Hells Angels. His friends, family, and Bandidos members all warned him to stop "posing" as a Hells Angels member and stop "shooting off his mouth" or he could get beaten up or killed. He continued. As predicted, he was killed on March 18, 2006. A sniper's bullet blew his brains out as he left an Austin pizza parlor with his girlfriend and his two small children. The speculation was that Bandidos killed the man who rode his motorcycle with a fake Hells Angels patch on his leather vest. There were no arrests, and the murder case lay dormant for 10 years until March 2017, when four Bandidos members were indicted for murdering the "fake" Hells Angel (Roundtree, March 5, 2017).

Public random outlaw biker violence affects anyone in the vicinity. In 2001, a 17-year-old youth was waiting in line at a Montreal nightclub when several Hells Angels members got into a fight with the person monitoring the door. One of the Angels pulled out a gun and started shooting. The youth was shot and killed. Several victims of outlaw biker violence attended his funeral—a journalist shot after writing articles critical of outlaw bikers, a Montreal crime reporter shot six times after writing a biker exposé, and a waitress shot four times as she was used as a human shield during a police–biker standoff (Peritz, October 26, 2001). Even shopping malls are not safe from random biker violence. An Australian woman who was shopping in a mall was wounded in the exchange when a fight between a Bandidos member and a former member erupted into gunfire (Mellor, September 30, 2014).

Random Violence Fueled by Alcohol and Other Drugs

Alcohol and other drugs common in the saloon society fuel the ever-present potential for violence. Few dispute that violence is a preferred "problem-solving" technique. Outlaw bikers are motivated by a common slogan "When in doubt, knock them out." There is no need for discussion or argument when the encounter can be solved with a punch and a kick. The well-known outlaw biker motto, "one on all, all on one," makes clear that if there is an encounter with a biker, all bikers present become engaged. Challenging an outlaw biker to a fair fight is not an option. If a "citizen" makes the challenge, all the bikers present in a biker bar may join in, whether or not they are in the same club. If a fight is lost or considered to indicate a "lack of respect," the likely "total retaliation" will be swift and often deadly.

Outlaw bikers can be dangerous and violent to anyone who intentionally or accidentally comes into contract with them, especially when they are fueled by alcohol or other drugs. In 1989, a drunk and "methed up" Fates Assembly MC member drove his car into a ditch and then shot to death a female neighbor who stopped to help him (www.onepercenterbikers.com). In 2001, a drunken grandmother was beaten, stabbed, and then buried in a shallow grave in the desert for disrespecting a drunken and "methed up" group of Mesa, Arizona, Hells Angels in their clubhouse. One of the HAMC members was a highly successful stockbroker, and another was a contract government-paid informant. In a bizarre twist on this case, the federal operative received no prison time for his part in the murder even though he admitted his guilt (Wagner, August 25, 2006).

Biker Domestic Violence

Domestic violence is a form of outlaw biker spontaneous expressive (violent) acts; however, there is limited research on the effects on women and children in the biker culture. Domestic violence does take place. This author's first encounter with domestic violence and outlaw bikers occurred in the 1960s involving a member of the Navy's Shore Patrol at the Naval Air Station in Meridian, Mississippi. There was a well-known brothel called "Ma Shoemaker's" on the outskirts of Meridian that was off-limits to military personnel. The patrol officers made frequent checks for sailors and marines. It was no secret that the Outlaws MC ran the brothel, nor that there was a link between the Outlaws MC and the Ku Klux Klan (KKK). The sex workers at the brothel confided in the patrol officers and asked for help against their abusive boyfriends, husbands, and pimps. They frequently complained about being forced into prostitution. As bruises, black eyes, and broken bones supported their claims, patrol officers reported the abuse to the local law enforcement authorities. Eventually, though, the women and young girls begged the patrol officers to stop reporting because of the retaliation they were receiving.

Seeking outside help for biker domestic violence is still dangerous. In Australia, a Bandidos member was sentenced in 2017 to life in prison for forcing his former domestic partner off the road and then beating her to death in the overturned car (https://meanwhileinoz.com.au). The woman had recently sought help from the police with regard to his repeated acts of domestic violence.

Bobby Nauss, the Warlocks MC sexual homicide serial killer, who will be discussed in more detail in the next chapter, struck his girlfriend in front of other bikers on their third date (Bowe, 1994). The abuse continued, with repeated attempts to break off the relationship, but she always came back. Nauss had her "pull the train" (submit to gang rape) with other Warlocks members when he was initiated into the gang. The abuse continued until one night after sexual intercourse when Nauss hanged her from a beam in a garage and took a friend to the hanging nude body and announced, "I killed her. I hung her. Now she won't bother me anymore" (Bowe, 1994: 9).

Forced sex among domestic partners is a common form of retaliation in the outlaw biker world. If a biker's "old lady" (i.e., exclusive sex partner or wife) is unfaithful with a non-biker, withholds money, or publicly embarrasses her "old man," she may have to "pull a train" or a "face train" (perform fellatio) (Quinn, 2007). An anal train is considered the most serious form of domestic sexual violence.

Domestic violence extends to children as well. Undercover ATF agent Jay Dobyns was offered the "services" of two minor females by an Arizona Hells Angels leader in 2009. One of the minors was the gangster's daughter.

Cooper and Bowden (2006) provide case studies on the physical and psychological effects on the women and children of bikies in Australia and the problems social workers face when dealing with them as clients. Sixteen percent of the women that were seen in the domestic violence clinic were women leaving bikies in gangs.

Sociopaths in the Outlaw Biker World

Outlaw biker spontaneous expressive violence includes violence directed at anyone who randomly encounters those who experience impulsive, irrational outbursts of violence. One Canadian Hells Angels leader, for example, was aptly nicknamed "Skitzo," and everyone associated with him was wary of his bizarre violent behavior (Dow, October 9, 2014). Reportedly, a 60-year-old neighbor found his dog wandering the streets and took the dog in. She placed "lost dog" posters throughout the neighborhood, and Skitzo called and demanded the dog back. He was so abusive to her that she refused unless he could prove he was the owner. The infuriated Hells Angel threatened to kill her. Finally, a local veterinarian vouched that the dog did belong to Skitzo, and she returned the pet. Skitzo then began a campaign of harassing the women with late-night calls, eventually showing up at her door one day to punch her in the face.

In San Diego, California, a 60-year-old man, along with his son and daughter-in-law, walked by several Hells Angels standing outside a sports bar (www.sandiego6.com). The Hells Angels began making inappropriate sexual remarks to the woman, and the man scolded them. One of the Angels, later identified as a chapter president, yelled that he was going to run over them. The trio continued walking, and the Hells Angels leader got in his car and struck the father-in-law, who was walking with a cane in the crosswalk, with his vehicle before speeding off. The victim suffered several broken bones and a collapsed lung. Witnesses followed the speeding assailant, and he was soon captured. The police located the perpetrator because he was on federal probation and wearing a GPS tracking device.

Another Hells Angels member, from Lynn, Massachusetts, was charged with a vicious attack on a citizen who tried to intervene in an altercation between the OMC/G member and his girlfriend's ex-husband (Manganis, December 30, 2014). The citizen required plastic surgery to sew his lower lip together after being hit with a sharpened ring worn by the Angel, a common weapon. The prosecutor called the Angel "a brutal, violent dangerous man" and cited earlier incidents where he had beaten an off-duty police officer and was charged with smashing a man's face into a car. The Salem District Court judge agreed with the prosecutor's characterization of him as a dangerous man.

The violent, sometimes savage, acts of outlaw bikers to rivals and others in the saloon society milieu, or those coming in contact for whatever reason with outlaw bikers, leads many to believe that the spontaneous expressive violent acts are the result of the personal pathology of the members (Quinn and Forsyth, 2011). However, social pathology seems to be a poor explanation for the spontaneous expressive violent acts of all or a majority of outlaw bikers.

A number of outlaw bikers have been documented as sociopaths or deranged individuals committing serial and multiple murders and sex crimes with no conscience and morality. A Canadian

HAMC hitman in the Montreal Biker War committed 43 murders for the club. At his sentencing, the judge remarked "You've killed more people than the Canadian army during the Gulf War" (Sanger, 2005: 333). During the same war, a hitman for the competing Rock Machine MC murdered 27 people. Although the previous two cases are examples of planned expressive violence against rival bikers, the serial nature of the murders indicates personal pathology. Other examples of murderers who fit into the sociopath category include "Taco" Bowman of the Outlaws MC, "Moms" Boucher of the Hells Angels, Don Chambers of the Bandidos MC, and numerous others. Serial sexual killers have been members of OMC/Gs. For example, Bobby Nauss of the Pennsylvania Warlocks MC, who was mentioned earlier in the chapter, as well as "Crazy" Joe Spaziano of the Hells Angels and Florida Outlaws MC. A former Outlaws MC member said of Crazy Joe Spaziano: "Everyone kept their distance from him. He was unpredictable. I think he enjoyed killing. He said the best sex he ever had was after killing someone" (Leusner and Griffin, January 8, 1996). While these examples may be aberrations, there is little doubt that the outlaw biker culture is violent and attracts and nurtures violent men.

Planned Expressive Violence

Planned expressive [violent] acts most often occur over "colors" or territory and crime markets. "Biker wars" exemplify this type of violence. These planned violent acts are used as a tool to deter witnesses. Internecine collective violence is used as an internal control technique for snitches or those who introduce an informant to the club. Quinn and Forsyth (2011) opine that constant internecine violence is one of the most dominant themes in biker life.

According to Kalogerakis, Quebec Superior Court Justice Gilles Hébert, at the sentencing hearing of a Hells Angels member, said "This violence has to be denounced with energy and the criminal organizations that base their violence have to be fought with determination and severity" (Kalogerakis, October 9, 2002).

The constant war mentality shaped the development of OMCs and the evolution to OMGs and the shifting alliances between and among OMC/Gs. This constant shifting of alliances increased the danger of outlaw biker life: one's friend today may be an enemy tomorrow. The outlaw biker world, especially at the local level, is a small one, and members of one club will know or have known the members of another club. The more recent practice of moving from one club to another enhances this familiarity.

In biker wars, the most savage members assume control as friends kill, maim, or injure "old friends" or former "brothers" who have turned against the club. The weak and timid who would be peacemakers are expelled from the club. A member goes along or gets out. Being a club member is a single full-time role for the patch holder, and giving it up is not easy. For those involved in organized criminal activities, war for rational purposes of profit through crime is just a matter of "taking care of business."

Biker Wars

While a separate chapter on biker wars (Chapter 7) will be presented later, some aspects of biker wars will be addressed here.

Long-Standing Hatred of Rivals

Planned expressive violence occurs because of long-standing hatred of one club for another. It can happen in any country with competing OMC/Gs. For example, a 51-year-old member of the Irish Road Tramps MC was shot dead outside the Road Tramps clubhouse by members of a rival Irish motorcycle club (Lally, June 22, 2015). The general violent acts against rival groups may have been planned some time before the specific acts occur.

Violence erupts whenever rival clubs meet. To wit, when the Victory Outreach Church of Los Banos, California, held a rally "to stop the violence" in their community (Albrecht, July 1, 2009), 10 members of the Mongols MC showed up and were invited to stay and eat some food. Shortly thereafter, seven or eight Hells Angels MC members showed up and started shouting at the Mongols, leading to shots being fired and bikers being stabbed. The crowd, which included children, ran for cover. The police made several arrests, and two victims went to the hospital. In another incident, two Pagans MC members were in a Baltimore County, Maryland, nightclub and were walking to the door to leave when a 6-foot-9-inch, 340-pound Hells Angels prospect and another man stepped in front of them. The Hells Angels prospect pulled a gun and started shooting, wounding both Pagans members (Barnhardt, January 6, 2004). The HAMC and the Pagans MC, who were bitter enemies, had a shoot-on-sight order among them. Another example can be found in a 2008 incident between the Mongols and the Hells Angels. The outlaw bikers had a chance meeting at the Special Memory Wedding Chapel in Las Vegas, Nevada, which resulted in a brawl that injured six people (Ferrara, February 6, 2015). The Mongols wedding party had been coming out as the Hells Angels wedding party was going in. Never missing a chance to fight, the groups went after each other. Similar seemingly random acts of violence have been reported across the country. In 2012, six members of the New Roc Hells Angels were indicted for beating a Diablos MC member in the head with a hammer in a Poughkeepsie, New York, restaurant, sending the other diners running in terror (U.S. Department of Justice, March 16, 2017). The Diablos had been encroaching on Hells Angels territory.

Chance encounters on the street can lead to outlaw biker violence. One biker was killed and two injured when Mongols and Hells Angels members began shooting at one another on a freeway off ramp in Riverside, California (Nelson, September 21, 2014). A street shootout between the Hells Angels and the Bandidos outside a club on New Year's Eve in 2015 in Dusseldorf, Germany, left a Hells Angels and an innocent person walking by gravely wounded (www.thelocal.de).

In fact, public shooting in public spaces frequently results in innocent deaths. A planned murder of a Montreal Bandidos leader went awry when a Hells Angels hit team searching for him shot to death an innocent man pumping gas at a service station (Peritz, March 16, 2002). The victim, a father of two, had the same kind of car as the intended victim.

Internecine Violence

Planned expressive internecine violence—that is, violence within the same group or "brother-hood" and orchestrated by the leaders and other members—is another form of violence. Joining any gang, whether a youth gang or an adult criminal gang, increases the likelihood of death from rivals or from one's peers (Barker, 2015b). A Vancouver, Canada, Hells Angels member who vouched for and introduced a police agent to the club was never seen again after nine members went to jail (Bolan, July 25, 2008). An Outlaws MC "enforcer" testified at the trial of Jack "Milwaukee Jack" Rosga, the international president, that Rosga ordered him to take revenge on a Hells Angel for the assault of two Outlaws in Connecticut (U.S. Department of Justice, December 21, 2010). Revenge included taking a vest or killing the Angels. The assault left the Angel alive but paralyzed. Outlaws MC members wear an ADIOS tattoo or patch, which is translated as "Angels Die in Outlaw States."

One bizarre instance of internecine violence occurred at the funeral of the president of the San Jose chapter of the Hells Angels. A member of the Vagos MC had killed him in a Sparks, Nevada, casino. There was a heavy police presence at the funeral, but that did not prevent what happened (Kaplan, October 15, 2016). The sergeant at arms of the Hells Angels San Jose chapter, known as MR 187 (the California penal code for murder), got in a fistfight with another HAMC member, accusing him of not protecting the slain HA leader. One Angel shot his Angel attacker dead and then fled the scene with help from his brothers. Violence, to the extreme, can occur anywhere and with anyone in the violent outlaw biker world.

The planned expressive acts are used as an internal control technique to enforce rules and punish violators, such as those who leave "out bad," which is discussed in Chapter 3. For example, three members of the Buffalo, New York, Chosen Few MC, including the club president, were accused of beating with bats and stealing the motorcycle of a man who wanted to leave the club (Herbeck, September 9, 2009). In an ironic case, a Vancouver Hells Angels debt collector was so brutal that he was kicked out of the gang for being too violent and then murdered (Bolan, August 13, 2010). It was felt that he was bringing too much attention to the Hells Angels. The police had met with the chapter president and told them that he was out of control, which sealed the man's "out bad" status and execution.

A confusing incidence of internecine, brother-on-brother murder occurred in San Bernardino, California, in 2017. According to newspaper accounts, three Vagos MC members were inside a bar when an altercation erupted (Yarborough, April 3, 2017). The fight moved out to the parking lot, leading to the deaths of two members at the hands of another member. One of the deceased was the president of the Vagos San Bernardino chapter. The third member left the scene on his bike and then later turned himself in to the San Bernardino Sheriff's office. He was charged with two counts of murder and held without bond. What happened next raises more questions than answers. According to *The Aging Rebel* blog, 34 hours after his arrest, the Vagos member was released without bail, and there is no record of the murders with the San Bernardino Superior Court. This has led to speculation that the case is closed (*The Aging Rebel*, April 7, 2017) and that the Vagos member who killed his fellow club members may have been a police informant.

Violence to Achieve Criminal Objectives

Planned expressive acts are also the means by which outlaw bikers use violence to enforce their criminal objectives. For example, the Crew MC, a puppet/support club of the British Columbia Hells Angels, used beatings, mutilations, and murder to collect debts and instill fear—one man had his finger cut off, and another lost a hand. OMGs often use hitmen or designated killers to advance their criminal agenda. One bizarre case involved the Rockers MC, an Ontario, Canada, Hells Angels puppet/support club, during the Montreal Biker War. The Rockers MC had two teams— the "baseball" team that beat people up and the "football team" that killed people. The Rockers used a bisexual pair of lovers—highly unusual for the usually homophobic bikers—on their football team (Hu, May 6, 2001). When the couple had a falling out, one became an informant and brought down the Hells Angels involved.

Outlaw clubs also use violence and the threat of violence to deter victims from reporting or testifying against them. The Victoria, Australia, police accused corrupt unions of using OMGs to collect debts and threaten witnesses, leading to witnesses not showing up to testify (Livingston, September 18, 2014). In Sweden, an Iranian immigrant, who was a Swedish citizen, was threatened. His two small children were also threatened and his car torched, and then he was forced to close his popular restaurant because of extortion threats from outlaw biker gangs (Ekman, July 11, 2007). A Bellingham, Washington, victim whose car was stolen by a Bandidos member was told that his family would be killed if he reported it (Millage, June 19, 2005). The wife of another witness in the same case was told, "Tell your husband to drop the charges or you won't wake up some morning" (Millage, June 10, 2005). The ATF spokesperson for this case said, "Bandidos are very clearly one of the most dangerous criminal organizations in the world."

Empirical Studies of Biker Violence

There is a plethora of books, articles, and other popular material on outlaw biker violence; however, there are a limited number of empirical research studies of biker violence available.

Few research studies on outlaw bikers using primary data are available because of the violent nature of the members of this secret deviant group (Barker, 2015a; Quinn and Forsyth, 2009). Face-to-face interactions with outlaw bikers is challenging and dangerous. Danner and Silverman (1986) conducted one of the first biker violence studies. The researchers compared the results of a survey administered to inmates in U.S. adult correctional institutions. One hundred and sixty-nine respondents out of a population of 410 returned the questionnaire—a response rate of about 41%. The inmate respondents were asked if motorcycles or cars were their preferred mode of transportation. Those who selected motorcycles were classified as "outlaw bikers," which is an obvious possible misclassification because not everyone riding a motorcycle is an outlaw biker even if they are incarcerated. In spite of this error, the study's results have value for understanding biker violence. Incarcerated "bikers" tended "to be white, and to be incarcerated for a violent offense" (Danner and Silverman, 1986: 62). Therefore, we have an indication that there may be a behavioral connection between those who ride motorcycles and those who do not. A limited number of other studies also suggest there is a link between bikers and violent behavior.

Barker and Human (2009) performed a content analysis of newspaper articles retrieved from the LexisNexis data source using the two categories of biker violence outlined in Quinn and Koch's study: *spontaneous expressive acts* and what Barker and Human term *planned aggressive acts* (based on Quinn and Koch's category of *planned expressive acts*). Barker and Human searched for articles mentioning the Big Four Motorcycle Clubs—the Hells Angels, Bandidos, Outlaws, and Pagans. The search fields were "all available dates" and "all available years." A total of 631 articles were identified: Outlaws MC (347), Hells Angels MC (209), Bandidos MC (50), and Pagans MC (25). The content analysis revealed that the articles discussed 59 separate incidents. Of that total, there were 18 *planned aggressive acts* and 17 *spontaneous expressive acts*. Not surprisingly, the HAMC had the most *planned aggressive acts*—10 (five in the United States, four in Canada, and one in Australia). The *planned aggressive acts* were all directed at club rivals and sanctioned by club leaders.

The HAMC has a well-deserved reputation of being the most violent OMG, a label they vehemently deny. The 17 *spontaneous expressive acts* were divided as follows: HAMC, four; Outlaws, six; Bandidos, six; and Pagans, one. The spontaneous expressive incidents were primarily individual or group fights or brawls taking place in a public setting.

Klement's (2016) research is a descriptive study of outlaw biker crime prevalence and frequency in Denmark. Using data supplied by the Danish National Police and the national statistical agency, Statistics Denmark, the author examined the prevalence and frequency of crimes committed by outlaw bikers (Hells Angels MC, Bandidos MC, and the indigenous No Names MC and their support clubs) from 2001 to 2013. At the time there were 1,404 outlaw bikers registered in the Police Intelligence Database (PID). The PID information is gathered from police outlaw and street gang squads and considered extremely reliable. Outlaw Motorcycle Gangs are considered a major priority for the Danish police; they are kept under tight surveillance and their criminal convictions are recorded in the PID. "Convictions for violent crimes" (assaults and threats) is one of the 12 categories of crimes recorded. Danish outlaw bikers are convicted for violent crimes more often than any of the other crime categories. In fact, the study found that violent crimes are commonplace among Danish outlaw bikers. Moreover, the study found that Danish bikers are involved in violent crimes long before being registered in the PID, suggesting that violent tendencies may be criteria for selection into the Outlaw Motorcycle Clubs. The study also found violence and criminal behavior increased after affiliation with an outlaw club.

The limited studies on outlaw biker violence suggest support for the accepted premise that OMC/Gs have the potential for violence from individual and group members—*spontaneous expressive acts*—and from the club or gang as a collective—*planned expressive or aggressive acts*. There is a critical need for additional scholarly research on the deviant and secret group that make up outlaw bikers. In the interim, it is instructive to examine how the participants in the outlaw biker world view themselves and the "clubs."

Views from the Inside

Since 2008, Donald Charles Davis has blogged about the Outlaw Motorcycle Club (OMC) world under the title *The Aging Rebel*. He writes about the "outlaw world from the point of view of the outlaws rather than the perspective of the police" (Davis, 2015a: 129). His blog posts are supportive of outlaw bikers and critical of law enforcement. The OMC world and its members, as "proper outlaws," according to Davis,

> keep their eyes and ears open and their mouths shut. They never testify against anybody. They are honor bound to only testify for the defense. With rare exceptions, they do not talk to reporters. They "handle their own business." Proper outlaws do not run from fights. When they fight they fight to win. They fight with their fists, with knives and guns.
>
> *(Davis, 2015a: 1–2)*

In fact, outlaw bikers are always prepared for violence (see Box 5.2).

Chuck Zito, a convicted felon (for drug conspiracy), also espouses the violent view of outlaw bikers. Zito is the former HAMC New York Nomads chapter president. He is also a media celebrity,

---

BOX 5.2 OUTLAW BIKERS' VIEW OF VIOLENCE

Motorcycle outlaws insist they own every bar they enter. They openly wear pistols, Bowie knives, ball peen hammers and collapsible batons. They wear improvised slapjacks, padlocks laced with folded and pressed bandannas in their back pockets. They wear heavy, sharp rings on their fingers, the better to break the bones in your face. If you fight one you will probably lose because they all know how to fight. But if you fight one you can't just fight one. You have to fight them all. They refuse to lose.

Source: Davis, 2015a: 187–188.

---

appearing in movies and the TV show *Sons of Anarchy*. Zito and coauthor Layden described the outlaw "culture of violence" succinctly: "When outlaw motorcycle clubs meet to settle a grievance and they're armed with guns, people can and do get hurt. It's part of the culture, part of the risk. It's also part of the appeal" (Zito and Layden, 2002: 90). Zito and Layden's book, *Street Justice*, is a continuous flow of one violent act after the other, including his own allegations of domestic violence. In 2002, Zito pleaded guilty to violating a protective order that prohibited him from contacting his wife. He said he would rather go to jail for 12 days than attend a "Workshop Against Violence" each week for a year. He told the judge, "I can't sit in a room with 10 to 12 men talking about how they beat their wives and kids" (Bandler, August 23, 2002).

Davis writes,

> For the last forty years motorcycle clubs have been a paramilitary fraternal organizations comprised of law-abiding Trump Republicans but they are violent as the Twin Peaks. The [2015 Waco, Texas, shootout] massacre was violent, as war is violent and as America has always been violent.
>
> *(Davis, 2015a: 60)*

Few familiar with the Outlaw Motorcycle Club world argue with his assessment of OMC/G violence. The one-percenter world is not politically correct. According to Hayes, "Censoring the name of a football team, waving a rainbow flag, or apologizing again for the Civil War doesn't cut any hard ice when MC's face off and *discuss* things" (Hayes, 2016: 21). Visitors and those who travel in the saloon society milieu must be careful.

Dave Nichols, the editor-in-chief of the premier motorcycle magazine *Easyriders*, advises all who travel in the outlaw biker milieu to tread softly in the presence of an outlaw biker (Nichols, 2012). He even cautions on how to look at an outlaw biker, "Never eye-fuck a one percenter [outlaw biker]. Don't challenge them with your eyes … or anything else for that matter. It will just get you thumped" (Nichols, 2012: 67). Nichols proposes a set of rules to be followed by those who come into casual contact with an outlaw biker (see Box 5.3).

BOX 5.3 RULES TO BE FOLLOWED WHEN IN THE PRESENCE OF A ONE-PERCENTER (OUTLAW BIKER)

- Never touch a one-percenter. Never touch a one-percenter's cut or patch. Even brushing by in a crowded room can get you beaten up.
- Never touch a one percenter's motorcycle unless you enjoy getting yourself a proper beating.
- Make sure your girlfriend never touches or sits on anyone's bike but your own.
- Don't think that wearing a support patch buys you anything. You are not a member. You are a civilian. Never wear a support shirt anywhere that a warring club can see, or you're dead meat.
- Keep your thoughts to yourself. Until you show yourself about being about something and not one of the walking dead (citizens), one percenters don't give a shit what you think.
- Never disrespect a one percenter's ol' lady (girlfriend or wife). Period.
- Never interrupt two or more patch holders when they are having a conversation. This is disrespectful.

Source: Modified from Nichols, 2012: 111.

Conclusion

The ever-present impulsive, often irrational violence, of outlaw bikers makes any encounter, however random, extremely dangerous and unpredictable. Alcohol and other drugs and a low tolerance for any indications of disrespect fuel this unpredictable violence. Showing "class" to one's brothers includes joining in on these violent encounters. As outlined, there are two general categories of outlaw biker violence: *spontaneous expressive (violent) acts* and *planned expressive/aggressive acts*. The following two chapters will provide selected examples of these two categories of outlaw biker violence: "bad men" and biker wars.

6

"BAD MEN" IN THE OUTLAW BIKER COMMUNITY

Introduction

As we have seen, violence in the extreme, including mass murder, is common in the outlaw biker world, where you have to be violent to protect yourself from violence. Violence is necessary to establish, protect, and defend club territory and illegal markets. Violence is necessary to make others fear you. If others don't fear you; you give up your patch. However, even within the violent outlaw biker culture, there are "bad men" who exceed the boundaries of "accepted" or "tolerated" violent behavior. They have been described as "bad to the bone" or "sick puppies."

Paradoxically, extreme violence for club purposes is exalted and rewarded in Outlaw Motorcycle Clubs/Gangs who reward members with special symbols and patches for violence, especially sanctioned violence against rivals or law enforcement officers. The Hells Angels award the Dequiallo [No Quarter] patch to those who assault or fight with law enforcement officers. The Outlaws MC dictates that "an Outlaw who commits murder, attempts murder, or explodes a bomb on behalf of the Outlaws is entitled to wear 'lightning bolts,' a Nazi-style 'SS' tattoo" (*United States* v. *Bowman*, 2002). The equivalent Hells Angels patch, the "Filthy Few" patch, is given to members who kill or commit violence for the club (Barker, 2007). Other OMC/Gs have similar patches. The Bandidos "Expect No Mercy" or "Bad Company" patch serves the same function to recognize those who kill or assault for the club. The 1%-er or diamond patch is giving to Wheels of Soul MC members who are particularly criminal or violent (*United States* v. *Wheels of Soul*, June 9, 2011). Furthermore, it is common for Outlaw Motorcycle Gangs to have squads to carry out planned aggressive violence. Examples are the Nomads chapters, the Rock Machine's "Dark Circle," or the "Inner Circle" of the Pennsylvania Warlocks MC.

The following cases represent a selection of OMC/G members who impulsively and randomly victimize persons in the saloon society, those they randomly encounter in or out of the saloon society milieu, and victims they seek out to prey on for personal reasons (often for illicit sexual motives). The chapter also examines some "bad men" who act on leaders' or club orders to kill, maim, and injure. As one outlaw biker said to this author years ago, "Man, _____ is one mean son of a bitch. Look at his eyes; there ain't nobody home." There are a lot of "mean sons of bitches" (MSOBs) in the outlaw biker culture. We begin with three MSOBs, all sexual homicide serial killers.

Selected "Bad Men"

MSOBs: Sexual Homicide Serial Killers and Rapists

Bobby Nauss, Pennsylvania Warlocks MC

Bobby Nauss is a well-rounded criminal—a thief, drug trafficker, rapist, and sexual homicide serial killer. His early background gave no indication of the heartless killer of young girls he became (Bowe, 1994). He was one of eight children, growing up in Darby, Pennsylvania. He was a Boy Scout and played Little League baseball; it seemed everyone thought he was a nice guy. This changed in high school. Nauss was not a good student in high school, preferring to work with his hands. His father was an automobile mechanic and trained him to be one as well. Bowe (1994) writes that after a break up with a girlfriend when he was 18, Nauss began drinking and then progressed to "shooting up" methamphetamine (meth). His meth use brought him into contact with outlaw bikers. Bobby bought a motorcycle and started "hanging around" in the Warlocks MC saloon society milieu.

At 19, Nauss joined the Warlocks MC and used his mechanic skills to steal cars. The Warlocks MC, as explained earlier, is an Outlaw Motorcycle Club that came into being in 1967 as an adult criminal gang, requiring members to commit serious crimes such as theft, rape, or murder. Nauss's criminal career included each type of felony. Each member is required to get three tattoos: a swastika, a naked woman, and the words "Born to Lose."

The inclusion of rape in the Warlocks' required crime list and the naked-woman tattoo indicate the contempt for females held by club members. To the Warlocks, women are considered throw-away sex objects. The Warlocks believe women exist to provide sexual gratification to men. As part of their initiation into the "club," the Warlocks demand new members provide a woman to "pull the train" of all members. Nauss didn't look too far for a victim—he fed barbiturates to his girlfriend and took the woozy woman to the clubhouse where his Warlocks brothers undressed her and raped her for two hours. She was emotionally and psychologically damaged from the experience. As noted in Chapter 5, later, Nauss hanged her. Nauss became a career criminal after joining the Warlocks. He also became a committed sadistic sexual predator.

Nauss's girlfriend had disappeared before he became a Warlocks member. He was the likely suspect in her disappearance. He soon became a suspect in other deaths and disappearances. Beginning in 1975, bodies of young girls from Darby began to appear, and other girls and women from close areas disappeared. Two young teenage girls—15 and 16 years of age—were found in a nearby river. Autopsies revealed they had been sexually molested and shot to death. Then, a 15-year-old girl from the borough next to Darby was found battered and unconscious with a plastic cord around her neck. The location was next to the railroad tracks, just four blocks from where Nauss worked. The victim told the police she was waiting for a bus when two men asked if she wanted a ride. She made a tragic mistake and said yes. They took her to an unknown location, beat her, injected her with meth, and raped her. She passed out and was left for dead.

Unfortunately, she was unable to give a description of the attackers. Almost a week later, another female teenager, a 17-year-old in the same neighborhood, got in a fight with her boyfriend and decided to walk home. She was never seen alive again. Several months later, a 20-year-old woman vanished.

In 1976, bodies, or what was left of them, were found in the marshes around the city of Darby. A pattern soon developed in the deaths and disappearances. The attacks were sexually related, involved drugs, and the specter of the Warlocks MC was in the background.

Nauss was directly connected to the next sexual assault. In October of 1976, Nauss and two other Warlocks picked up a 21-year-old female acquaintance at her apartment. They had singly and as a group had sex with her on several occasions in the past. The partygoers stopped at a liquor store and bought two quarts of vodka. The next stop was a store where they bought plastic cups and ice. So equipped, they proceeded to a friend's apartment (the friend was at work). The "party" turned into a night of 25 forced deviant sex acts with four different men. Later, the victim testified in court, "I'd rather have been dead than go through what I did that night" (Bowe, 1994: 121). She reported the attack to the police, and the Warlocks members and Nauss's brother-in-law were arrested. While the sex attacks were going on, Nauss had called his brother-in-law and invited him to join in. During the investigation, a fellow Warlocks member "ratted out" Nauss for the murder of his missing girlfriend, saying that one night Nauss came into his bedroom and took him to an attached garage where the girlfriend's nude body hung from a beam. According to the witness, Nauss proudly announced, "I killed her. I hung her. Now she won't bother me anymore" (Bowe, 1994: 9).

Although the body of the missing woman was never found, Nauss was tried for her murder. Testifying at his trial, Nauss spun the tale that his girlfriend had hanged herself and that he was only guilty of getting rid of the body with the help of his friend. However, he had publicly told enough people he killed her, and hearing that, the jury was unconvinced by Nauss's explanation. He was convicted. Nauss was not tried for the other murders he was suspected of; the evidence was there, but his life sentence made additional trials unnecessary. It was over—or at least that is what everyone thought.

In 1983, five years into his life sentence, Nauss and another inmate escaped from prison with the help of a prison worker and Warlocks members on the outside. A lengthy search turned up nothing. In 1988, after being featured in two episodes of the show *America's Most Wanted*, Nauss was recaptured in Luna Pier, Michigan. He seemed to be leading a respectable life. He was married and the father of three. He was not working but appeared to have a lot of money from investments. However, that was not true. Nauss was operating a major methamphetamine trafficking organization for the Warlocks MC while on the run—still, it appears, "bad to the bone." Nauss is currently back in prison, as of this writing. The bodies of some of his victims are still missing.

Joseph "Crazy Joe" Spaziano, Florida Outlaws MC

"Crazy Joe" Spaziano, a member of the Outlaws MC, was a sadistic sex murderer at the top of anyone's list of MSOBs. He bragged to fellow outlaw bikers that sex was best after committing murder and that sexual satisfaction came with the pain to others. Rape and sexual mutilation appeared to be his favorite acts.

In 1973, a 19-year-old single mother, down on her luck with a deformed infant, took up Spaziano on his offer to live with him rent-free (Griffin and Leusner, December 17, 1995). The woman lived to regret that decision, but many others did not live after coming in contact with "Crazy Joe" of the Outlaws MC. This woman became just one of several women who were the property of the Florida Outlaws MC for the next 17 months. She said, "I was the moneymaker [prostitution and dancing topless in Orlando, Florida, bars and clubs]. That's what he always said. What's yours is mine, and what's mine is mine—including your son" (Griffin and Leusner, December 17, 1995). She described Spaziano as a short (5 foot, 5 inches) vicious man who paced the floor at night worrying about going to the electric chair. She said he disappeared for hours and sometimes came home bloody.

She described a scene at the Outlaws Orlando clubhouse reminiscent of the pre–Civil War slave markets. The Outlaws members brought their "property" women to the clubhouse where they were bought, sold, and traded. She described comforting a young woman who was crying because she was afraid she would be killed if she didn't give in to their demands to "turn tricks." She never saw the woman again and assumed she was killed.

The woman later went to Chicago with Spaziano as he fled to avoid arrest on a Florida rape charge. Spaziano was accused of brutally raping a 16-year-old student, stabbing her 12 times in her eyes (causing the loss of one eye), and then strangling her with her belt and leaving her for dead (Salamone and Leusner, May 5, 1996). In Chicago, Spaziano became an enforcer for the Chicago Outlaws MC. It is alleged that he and another Outlaws MC member killed a fellow club member and his girlfriend for violating club rules against heroin use (Griffin and Leusner, December 17, 1995). These murders are categorized as internecine violence for internal rule enforcement. After the murders, Spaziano's "ol' lady" said he kept saying, "If they catch me, I'll get the electric chair for this," and "We told them to not to do the damn heroin." It is not uncommon for those who sell illegal drugs to forbid their use, especially injectable drugs; drug traffickers know users can't be trusted. Spaziano was a suspect in two other Chicago murders before he was arrested and sent back to Florida on the rape warrant. Back in Florida, Spaziano was found guilty of the rape and sentenced to life in prison.

Spaziano's fellow outlaw biker buddies seemed to be terrified of this homicidal killer. One Outlaws brother, who was in the witness protection program, gave testimony of Spaziano killing two hitchhikers on different occasions (Griffin and Leusner, December 17, 1995). In the first encounter, Spaziano picked up a male hitchhiker and grabbed a hatchet from under the seat and buried it in the hitchhiker's skull. The second hitchhiker was a female who he shot in the back as she got out of the car. Spaziano told the witness that she screamed so loud that he got out of the car and stabbed her to death. He left a personalized knife in her back and had to go back and get it.

Following his rape conviction, Spaziano was convicted of another previously unsolved case: the brutal rape and murder of an 18-year-old medical clerk in a rural area near Orlando, Florida. When the victim's body was finally found, it was too decomposed to determine a cause of death. The only evidence against Spaziano was the testimony of a 16-year-old Outlaws wannabe who hung around with him. The teenager testified that he was with Spaziano when he took him to the burial site that contained two bodies, and Spaziano confessed killing them. The prosecutor admitted there was no case without the young witness. The witness said that Spaziano bragged about mutilating the woman's genitals while she was alive (Barstow, February 25, 1996). The jury recommended life imprisonment, but the judge rejected that and sentenced him to death.

Twenty years later, after five execution dates were set and stopped, it was learned that the recollections of the witness, who had been described by some as a "confused flake," came after being hypnotized. Hypnotism is a controversial interrogation technique, and its results were ruled inadmissible (Mello, 2001). The witness later recanted his testimony, and Spaziano was granted a new trial. Following several appeals and the setting of a new trial date for the murder, Spaziano pleaded "no contest" and was sentenced to time served—23 years. He appealed the earlier rape conviction without success and remains in prison on that sentence (Salamone, June 11, 1997). While some may doubt his guilt for the murder of the young medical clerk, without a doubt, "Crazy Joe" Spaziano lived, as one reporter described it, "a misfit's life of spontaneous brutality and murder" (Barstow, February 25, 1996). As the outlaw bikers say, "He was one mean son of a bitch."

Malcolm Rewa, New Zealand Highway 61 MC

Malcolm Rewa, a New Zealand outlaw biker—sergeant at arms (enforcer)—was a "bad man" among bad men. In 1998, he was sentenced to 22 years in prison for 24 rapes out of the 27 of which he was accused. One of his victims died during the brutal rape, which added 14 years to his sentence. In a bizarre twist, Rewa was convicted of raping the woman but not murdering her. A 17-year-old prospect for another OMC/G, for some reason, confessed to the murder two years after it was committed and spent 21 years in prison before being released and exonerated. Rewa's life history reads like a fiction horror story.

Rewa, who was convicted of stealing a woman's underwear when he was only nine, continued in a pattern of burglaries until he joined the army at 21, a stint that lasted only 18 months before he was discharged and committed his first known rape attempt (Crime.co.nz, n.d.). His wife at the time was in labor, and he broke into the home of a nurse at the hospital where his wife was being attended to and tried to rape her. He left behind incriminating evidence that led to his identification and capture. He pleaded guilty and was sentenced to 4.5 years in prison. The police speculate that his easy identification, arrest, and conviction led to extreme efforts to conceal his crimes thereafter. His final rape arrest was almost a decade later.

Rewa's rapes and attempts to sexual assault victims were known by his biker colleagues, and they continued after he joined the Highway 61 MC. In fact, his outlaw biker gang affiliation expanded his pool of vulnerable victims in the saloon society milieu. Rewa was a true sexual predator. His rapes were often not opportunistic, but instead he "hunted" and selected many of his victims. Although his victims ranged in age from 15 to 43, the majority of his known and suspected victims were attractive, young, single professionals who lived alone; not once was there a man in the house (Crime.co.nz, n.d.). He also chose some of his victims from women he or his wife knew; he wore a variety of disguises during these acquaintance assaults. All the victims noted that he had a small penis and had difficulty sustaining an erection. His erectile dysfunction frustration appear to have caused him to become more violent as erection problems continued during the assaults. One victim was beaten with a baseball bat. Sexual assault investigators report (based on personal experience and formal and informal interviews with working and retired police officers) that failure to get and sustain an erection and becoming violent are common among rapists and other sexual assaulters.

Although random selection of victims did not fit his typical pattern, the sexual assault that ended his reign of terror was opportunistic. A 15-year-old girl was walking her dog when Rewa attempted to abduct her and pull her into his vehicle. The young girl fought back and was severely assaulted, resulting in a broken nose, black eyes, and the need for metal plates to be inserted in her jaw. Her screams alerted her father, who got the tag number of Rewa's car as it sped away. This led to the first arrest since his initial attack nine and a half years earlier. At his 1998 trial, it took three months to present all the evidence. The jury deliberated 40 hours over four days before finding him guilty of 16 rapes of 13 women—some women were raped more than once. There are additional allegations of other rapes and sexual assaults against women who hung around with Rewa and his biker friends, but the police did not investigate them because they felt the victims were not credible.

Brutal Violent Men

Yves "Apache" Trudeau, Canadian Hells Angels MC

Yves "Apache" Trudeau, a Canadian Hells Angels MC hitman, known as "The Mad Bumper" and "The Mad Bomber," is the most prolific murderer in outlaw biker history. The diminutive (standing 5 feet, 6 inches, and weighing only 135 pounds) "killing machine" was definitely "bad to the bone"—a mass murderer and sex offender. Trudeau, leader of the infamous "North Chapter" of the Hells Angels in Sherbrooke, Ontario, admitted to murdering 43 people from September 1973 to July 1985—29 with guns, 10 with bombs, three with baseball bats, and one strangled (Everett, October 26, 2013). He is implicated in more than 40 murders in which he played a supporting role (driver, disposing of the body, etc.). Killing people was his job. His victims include the following:

- Jean-Marie Viel, shot to death in 1970 after stealing a motorcycle from a member of the North Chapter (this is supposedly Trudeau's first victim).
- Jeanne Desjardins, a grandmother killed in February 1980 for trying to help her son, an ex–Hells Angel member. Trudeau beat her to death and then killed her son and his girlfriend. He dumped their bodies in the St. Lawrence River.
- A member of the Outlaws MC and his girlfriend, who were blown up in 1980 when a bomb attached to the Outlaws member's motorcycle exploded.
- A member of the West End Gang (an Irish organized crime group), who was killed when a bomb planted in his car exploded. This murder was a "hit" for hire by the leader of the West End Gang.
- A brother-in-law of a Montreal Italian Mafia member, who was shot to death in 1983. This was a contract "hit" from the Montreal Mafia.
- A fellow member of the HAMC North Chapter, who was killed by Trudeau because he had a heavy drug problem and owed $150,000 in drug money to the club.
- A mass murder by Trudeau that took place in 1984 in retaliation for the murder of an HAMC member. Trudeau had a television that was packed with explosives delivered to the apartment where the four killers of the HAMC member lived. When the television exploded in the downtown apartment, it killed all four of them, injured eight innocent civilians, and knocked a big hole in the apartment building (https://gangstersout.blogspot.com).

The Hells Angels Motorcycle Club recognized Trudeau's killing skills with the awarding of the first Canadian "Filthy Few" patch for murder or violence. However, his flame of fame died out. The biker who started Quebec's first Outlaw Motorcycle Club, the Popeyes MC, which evolved into the first Canadian Hells Angels chapter, found himself on the HAMC hit list.

On March 24, 1985, eight leaders of the North HAMC chapter were invited to meet with HAMC leaders in Lennoxville, a borough of the city of Sherbrooke, Quebec. When they arrived, five were shot to death by an HAMC hit squad, and their bodies were dumped in the Hells Angels "graveyard," the St. Lawrence River. The surviving members were stripped of their patches and thrown out of the club. Trudeau was on the list of those to be killed, but he escaped that fate. Though he was invited to the meeting, he could not attend because he was in a Montreal detox center trying to get his cocaine addiction under control. The North Chapter fell out of favor with the Canadian HAMC leaders for their heavy drug use and using more drugs than they were selling. Internecine murder is a swift and sure control option common to OMC/Gs.

Realizing there was a murder contract on him, Trudeau became a police informant. He was the first Canadian Hells Angels member to become one. As part of his agreement to testify against his former "brothers," he was allowed to plead guilty to 43 counts of manslaughter (Everett, October 26, 2013). The manslaughter charges allowed for parole after seven years. His cooperation with the authorities provided information on 100 murders and led to 20 arrests.

Released on parole after serving seven years, Trudeau was given a new identity and led a secret life doing odd jobs. However, 10 years later, the "bad to the bone" murderer was arrested. He pleaded guilty to six counts of sexual exploitation, sexual interference, and sexual touching of a male victim under the age of 14, all taking place within a four-year period. The now convicted child molester returned to prison. Four years later, Trudeau was again paroled. This parole was granted to allow him to receive treatment for a terminal case of bone marrow cancer. He died of cancer in 2008.

Toby Mitchell, Australian Bandidos MC

Toby Mitchell was an Australian Bandidos MC Enforcer. With "Sergeant at Arms" and "Bad Company" tattooed on the left side of his head, Toby Mitchell, who was also a champion kick boxer, seems to be proud of how violent he is. This heavily tattooed man with metal front teeth survived two shootings, one in which he was shot six times. In the first shooting in 2011, Mitchell was on life support for a week; he lost a kidney and most of his liver. The second shooting involved an ambush outside a fortified Bandidos-affiliated motorcycle club. Mitchell and his drinking entourage arrived in three cars and were immediately fired on by a hit team following them. Mitchell received a bullet wound to his biceps (Silvester, March 4, 2013). Speculation is that a jail gang, the Prisoners of War, orchestrated this shooting because the Bandidos were encroaching on their debt collecting and nightclub security businesses.

"Too bad to die," Mitchell's injury from the first shooting and the second attempt on his life has not slowed down his criminal lifestyle. He was recently convicted of threatening to kill a man and his baby daughter over a disputed debt. In another incident, in a fit of road rage, Mitchell drove his vehicle at a cyclist in the bike lane then got out and punched the man in the face and drove off (Huffadine and Crane, September 25, 2015).

Caius Veiovis, Massachusetts Hells Angels MC Prospect

Sometimes the truth is so bizarre that it appears to be fiction; this is one of those times. In 2008, Roy Gutfinski Jr. was serving seven years in prison for assault with a razor in a blood-drinking ritual when he decided to legally change his name to Caius Veiovis (http://abc13/news), taking the name Veiovis, supposedly, after a legendary Italian vampire of the 1100s. Veiovis, whose nickname is "Trash," is a self-proclaimed vampire and Satanist. The violent Angels prospect had two rows of subdermal implants placed in his forehead so he would look like the devil.

Veiovis was convicted of the murder and torture of three men in 2011. At his trial in 2014, his last words to the judge and jury were, "I'll see you all in hell. Remember that, every fucking one of you, I'll see you all in hell" (Spencer, September 26, 2014). While Veiovis may end up in hell, first, he has to serve three consecutive prison sentences in Massachusetts.

A Hells Angels prospect, Veiovis was charged with helping two men, one a Hells Angels member, kidnap, murder, and dismember three men in August 2011. The third member of this vicious cabal was an Aryan Brotherhood member. The Hells Angels member was the sergeant at arms of the Berkshire, Massachusetts, Hells Angels chapter, who had previously beaten one of the murdered men with a baseball bat, forcing him to sign ownership of his truck over to his attacker. A fourth person charged with being an accessory claimed that he was forced to help dispose of the bodies. That man was given immunity for testimony. Supporting once again the Hells Angels saying, "Three can keep a secret if two of them are dead," the other two men were killed because they witnessed the kidnapping (Farberov, September 10, 2014). The two murdered witnesses happened to be "in the wrong place at the wrong time."

Paul Merle Eischeid, Arizona Hells Angels MC

According to court records, in October 2001, members of the Mesa, Arizona, Hells Angels chapter were having a party at their clubhouse when a group decided to go out and find women to join the party (*The Aging Rebel*, February 22, 2012). Cynthia Garcia, a 44-year-old mother of six who was a frequent visitor to the clubhouse, accepted the invitation. As the party progressed and the Angels indulged in methamphetamine, the clearly intoxicated woman started "mouthing off" at the Hells Angels, a serious taboo in biker culture. She was warned to stop, but continued. The senior Hells Angels member present, who also happened to be a paid informant for the ATF, knocked her off her stool and told three members to "take care of her." This meant stomping on her head repeatedly until she was bleeding and unconscious. The attackers tossed her into the trunk of a car and took her into the desert, where the beating continued. After the beating, Garcia was not dead, so they took turns stabbing her and cutting her throat, almost decapitating her, and leaving her to rot as they drove off.

One of the three Hells Angels involved in this assault was Paul Merle Eischeid, a "methed up," but otherwise clean-cut and outwardly respectable Charles Schwab stockbroker. Two years after the murder, Eischeid and other HAMC members involved in the killing were indicted as part of Operation Black Biscuit, a federal RICO investigation. Eischeid was charged with a Violent Crime in Aid of Racketeering (VICAR), namely, the murder of Cynthia Garcia (*United States* v. *Eischeid*, December 19, 2003).

Eischeid's bail hearing on December 19, 2003, was curious. The government presented its case for detention with this statement:

The Government asserts three grounds in support of its contention that Defendant Eischeid is a danger to the community: (1) the nature and seriousness of the charge against him murder as a VCAR [aka VICAR]; (2) the circumstances surrounding the murder, including the fact that Cynthia Garcia was beaten brutally, taken to a remote desert location, stabbed repeatedly, left to die, and her body was not found until six days later; and (3) the fact that Defendant Eischeid is a member of the Hells Angels Motorcycle Club ("HAMC"), members of which have been charged with various racketeering crimes in the Indictment, including attempted murder, drug trafficking, and witness tampering. The Government contends that Defendant Eischeid is a flight risk because of the severity of the charge pending against him and the fact that it could potentially result in a death sentence.

Eischeid's response to the statements was as follows:

Defendant Eischeid has identified a number of factors in support of his argument that he is not a danger to the community or a flight risk: (1) he has only a minimal criminal history (one dismissed misdemeanor); (2) he owns two homes in the Phoenix area; (3) he has lived in Arizona for 11 years; (4) he is employed, and has been employed for the last several years in responsible jobs; (5) he has a retirement savings account; (6) he is a college graduate from an Arizona university; and (7) he does not abuse drugs or alcohol.

The Court agreed with the defendant's assertions with respect to his level of danger to the community, and concluded as follows:

Defendant Eischeid will be released on conditions calculated to assure his appearance at trial and the safety of the community. These will include electronic monitoring, an order that he not affiliate with members of the HAMC or wear HAMC colors or identifying information, and an order that he not possess firearms of any kind before trial. The Court will reconsider this Order on the presentation of evidence that Defendant is in fact posing a … threat to others within the community or is a serious flight risk.

Out on bond, Eischeid proceeded to remove his ankle monitor and fled to Argentina, using a forged passport. In June 2011, a Hells Angels associate pleaded guilty to applying for a passport in 2004, using false information, and giving it to Eischeid (King, December 2, 2011). The associate was sentenced to nine months in prison. In 2007, Eischeid was added to the U.S. Marshal's 15 Most Wanted List. He was captured in Buenos Aires, Argentina, in 2011 after being on the run for eight years.

In 2012, Kevin J. Augustiniak, a second Hells Angels member involved in the same brutal murder, pleaded guilty to second-degree murder and was sentenced to 23 years in prison (Hendley, March 30, 2012). The leader (and ATF informant), Michael Christopher "Mesa Mike" Kramer, who, in effect, ordered the murder, pleaded guilty to manslaughter. He did not serve any time in prison and was placed in the U.S. Marshal's Witness Relocation Program. According to *The Aging Rebel* blog, Kramer was paid an average of $60,000 a year to testify against his brother Angels. It is reported that he received somewhere in the neighborhood of $197,000 for his cooperation (*The Aging Rebel*, February 22, 2012). There are also allegations that Kramer, who reportedly was a known methamphetamine addict as well as a former member of the Dirty Dozen Motorcycle Club before it patched over to the Hells Angels, was the principal assailant of Cynthia Garcia in the Hells Angels clubhouse. The final remaining member of the killing group was run over by Kramer and killed. Although Kramer claims it was an accident, the circumstances are suspicious.

Outlaw Biker Bosses

Hells Angels MC

Ralph "Sonny" Barger

If there is a "boss of bosses" in the outlaw biker world, it is the iconic HAMC leader Ralph "Sonny" Barger, self-proclaimed as "an American legend" (www.sonny barger.com). Barger metaphorically "sucks the air out of the room" anywhere and everywhere he goes—book signings, motorcycle rallies, HAMC meetings (local, regional, national, and international), and even courtrooms. Through the years, numerous bikers (not all OMC/G members) have whipped out their pictures taken with "the boss" with pride. This phenomenon extends even to law enforcement officers; the adulation is palpable.

In his autobiography, Barger tells of growing up in a dysfunctional family. His mother left when he was four years old. He claims to have had several suspensions for assaulting teachers and "liking" to fight, but not for being a bully or a delinquent (Barger, Zimmerman, and Zimmerman, 2000). Although he claims to have never killed anyone—his gun jammed on his only attempt, he claims—he ordered and participated in violent events, some resulting in fellow and rival bikers going to their "dirt bed," a biker saying for death. By his own admission, Barger lists 21 arrests from April 1957 to June 1987 (Barger, Zimmerman, and Zimmerman, 2000: 257–259), not counting other arrests outside of that period. Five of those arrests were for violence-related offenses, and there were also arrests for kidnapping, drug trafficking, and racketeering. In 1988, Barger and another Hells Angels member were convicted of conspiring to blow up the Louisville, Kentucky, Outlaws MC clubhouse. He served four years in a federal prison for that offense.

Barger was involved in or responsible for a variety of crimes. In 1968, the first known club-sanctioned execution of an HAMC member occurred when the member was force-fed barbiturates (i.e., "downers") after being convicted by a club "kangaroo court" for stealing HAMC president Barger's coin collection. Also in 1968, members of the Unknowns MC had the temerity to steal Barger's motorcycle, "Sweet Cocaine." Barger described their punishment:

> When we found the last guy, the punishment began. One at time we bullwhipped them and beat them with spiked dog collars, broke their fingers with ball peen hammers [this is a favorite biker weapon, which is legal to carry]. One of them screamed at us, "Why don't you just kill us and get it over with?"
>
> Then we took their motorcycles, sold them, and disbanded their club. Moral of the story—don't get caught stealing a Hells Angels bike, especially if it's the president's
>
> *(Barger, Zimmerman, and Zimmerman, 2000: 65)*

In 1969, the Hells Angels were paid $500 worth of free beer to provide security at the Altamont Free Concert, headlined by The Rolling Stones. Barger claims during the extreme violence, including the stabbing death of an 18-year-old black man by Angels, he kicked a "fat girl" in the face to prevent her from climbing on the stage and then when Rolling Stones member Keith Richards threatened to quit playing if the Hells Angels did not stop their violent acts, he took the following action: "I stood next to him [Richards] and stuck my pistol into his side and told him to start playing his guitar or he was dead. He played like a motherfucker." (Barger, Zimmerman, and Zimmerman, 2000: 165).

Barger is a media celebrity. He is author of five books; including his best-selling autobiography. He has appeared in movies (*Hell Angels on Wheels* (1967), *Hell's Angels '69* (1969)) and TV shows (*Sons of Anarchy*, as Lenny "The Pimp" Janowitz), and is arguably the most well-known outlaw biker in the world. However, there are warts on his pop culture façade. Barger is a convicted felon, an ex-con (with 13 years of prison time), a former cocaine addict, and an admitted drug dealer and violence-prone individual. His trusted ally for years, George Christie—now a disgraced former Hells Angels member—also accuses him of being an abuser of his wife and 14-year-old stepdaughter (Christie, 2016). In fairness, it is important to remember that Christie was expelled from the Hells Angels as "out bad, no contact" in 2011. He has been called "a liar, thief, a snitch and a con man" (*The Aging Rebel*, September 5, 2015).

However, it is not likely that Barger will be remembered for his personal acts of violence. History will instead remember him as the outlaw biker responsible for making the Hells Angels Motorcycle Club the largest and most violent outlaw biker gang in the world.

Sonny Barger (born October 8, 1938) is sometimes mistakenly referred to as the founder of the Hells Angels MC, but he was just 10 years old when the HAMC was founded in 1948. Barger dropped out of school in the tenth grade and joined the army in 1955 at age 16, using a fake birth certificate (Barger, Zimmerman, and Zimmerman, 2000). Less than a year later, he was discharged when his true age was discovered. He returned to his home in Oakland, California, and joined a "free-wheeling" motorcycle club, the Panthers. The Panthers were a wild bunch of young toughs who considered themselves outlaw bikers and acted the part. He left these "outlaws" and joined a group of outlaws looking for an identity. One of the group "wore a modified Air Force-like patch he found in Sacramento [in a burned-out dump], a small skull wearing an aviator cap inside a set of wings" (Barger, Zimmerman, and Zimmerman, 2000: 30). The group thought the patch was "cool" and decided to call themselves the Nomads Hells Angels after the patch. A fortuitous encounter with a real Hells Angels member began the modern era of the HAMC.

Sonny Barger met another biker wearing the same patch and learned that the original HAMC was formed in San Bernardino in 1948, and there were a number of autonomous and loosely affiliated Hells Angels chapters throughout Southern California (Barker, 2015a). These chapters had a basic organizational structure, and rules, regulations, and procedures for becoming a Hells Angels charter (chapter). The Oakland Hells Angels became an official Hells Angels charter on April Fools' Day in 1957 and would go on to become the HAMC's "mother chapter"—the world HAMC headquarters. Barger became President of the Oakland Chapter. He introduced new rules about new members, club officials, and induction of new charter/chapters. Under his leadership, the HAMC in the mid-1960s began expanding throughout the United States, and he became President of the National Hells Angels Motorcycle Club. International expansion was next.

The HAMC expanded into Canada, Australia, and then England. Barger eventually became International President of the Hells Angels Motorcycle Club. The shrewd Barger turned the HAMC into a nonprofit organization devoted to motorcycle safety and sold 500 shares (Martin, December 2, 1992). The logo was trademarked, and official Hells Angels support gear is sold worldwide online and at motorcycle conventions. The HAMC became the largest and most well-known OMC in history with Barger at the helm.

Maurice "Mom" Boucher

Maurice "Mom" Boucher was the ruthless and violent leader of the Montreal Nomads Hells Angels chapter during the deadliest organized crime war in history: the Quebec Biker War. A career criminal raised in poverty, Boucher left school in the ninth year and began a life of crime and drug addiction. At age 21 Boucher was convicted of three burglaries and served six months in prison (www.onepercenterbikers.com). Less than a year from his release, Boucher was convicted of armed robbery and sentenced to 40 months in prison.

Boucher's professed lifetime ambition was to become a full-patched Hells Angels member. His first step toward that goal started with his own club, the SS, a white supremacist motorcycle club, in consort with fellow criminal Salvatore Cazzetta. The SS club members were petty criminals who sold drugs and hijacked trucks. Cazzetta would later found the Rock Machine MC and become Boucher's major antagonist in the Quebec Biker War (Sher and Marsden, 2006). Sher and Marsden (2006) provide the best explication of the rise and fall of the Quebec Hells Angels. What follows is based on their seminal work. Incidentally, they consider Boucher to be more vicious than "Apache" Trudeau, discussed earlier in the chapter.

Boucher joined the HAMC in 1987 at a time when the local Quebec chapters were decimated by local and Royal Canadian Mounted Police (RCMP) actions. Boucher, a natural-born leader, joined forces with Hells Angels visionary, Walter "Nurget" Stadnick, who was determined to bring Canada under the banner of the Hells Angels and stamp out all competing Outlaw Motorcycle Gangs. Boucher was the field general leading the Hells Angels in war, and Stadnick was the diplomat working behind the scenes. These two conspirators almost succeeded, except the extreme violence they started brought them down.

For their plan to succeed, Boucher and Stadnick had to first control the drug trafficking in Quebec. Boucher and Stadnick created seven Hells Angels chapters in Quebec Province. The most powerful chapter was the Montreal Nomads chapter, which was led by Boucher and Stadnick. The 11 members of the Nomads began a campaign of total elimination of all gangs and criminal organizations involved in drug dealing in Quebec. Violence was their means to control. Bombs and drive-by shootings became a regular occurrence in Montreal. At first, the police ignored this criminal-on-criminal violence. The Montreal homicide commander is quoted as saying, "They're killing each other. I give a hell if some guy pops somebody who just got out of jail? No. We didn't give a shit" (Sher and Marsden, 2006: 312). This attitude changed, however, as it always does when violence occurs in a public space and innocents are killed or injured.

Eleven-year-old Daniel Desrochers was playing with a friend on a playground near the street when a bomb placed in a Jeep outside a Montreal biker hangout 50 yards down the street exploded. The Jeep driver, a local drug dealer, was killed instantly. A tiny piece of shrapnel from the bomb pierced little Daniel's skull, and he died four days later. The public reaction to the boy's death was intense. How could the authorities allow biker violence that placed ordinary citizens in danger? Local politicians responding to the public outcry responded in typical knee-jerk reaction. They demanded action and put millions of dollars into a police task force called Wolverine. They announced that the bikers' days were numbered, and then they resumed normal activities.

Operation Wolverine was a total disaster. Instead of fighting outlaw bikers, the cops on the task forces from different agencies fought with each other over control, assignments, and "who gets the credit" issues—a common problem with "cooperative" police operations. The Montreal police department pulled its officers off the task force, and a royal commission looking into the provincial police department, the Sûreté du Québec (SQ), began. The commission found the SQ racked by corruption and incompetence. Task Force Wolverine was no more. This prompted federal authorities, the RCMP, to step in.

The RCMP ran a separate anti-biker gang operation for years, with the aid of disgruntled biker Dany Kane. Kane became a paid informant and infiltrated the Nomads chapter several years before the Wolverine task force was created. He operated efficiently for three years and then went rogue as a hitman for the Nomads. He and his lover, Aimé Simard (the homosexual relationship was highly unusual for the generally homophobic biker culture), were involved in at least three murders. The operation "blew up" when Simard was arrested for three contract murders and informed on Kane. Kane was arrested, charged with murder, and sent to prison. Simard was murdered in prison, presumably for being a "rat." At that point, with the RCMP operation in shambles, the Nomads continued their elimination campaign.

Boucher took the bold action of retaliating against the government. He drew up a "hit" list of judges, prosecutors, politicians, journalists, police officers, and prison workers. His paid assassins murdered two prison guards and wounded a third in the summer of 1987. The prison guards chosen at random included a mother of four shot on her way home from work and a male worker ambushed when he stopped his empty prison bus at a railway crossing.

One of the prison guard assassins was caught, confessed, and agreed to testify against Boucher. The trial ended up being a travesty. Hells Angels members in full-patched colors showed up, paid those sitting in the front two rows for their seats, and then spent their time glaring at the jury—an attempt at jury intimidation. Boucher's lawyer, seemingly with the judge's help, refuted the testimony of the paid assassin. The jury found Boucher not guilty on all counts. The night of the trial's end, Boucher showed up at a boxing match in full colors, just as he predicted he would. He received a standing ovation. Maurice "Mom" Boucher was now a folk hero emboldened by his acquittal. The carnage continued. A leading Montreal crime reporter, after writing a series of derogatory stories about Boucher and his killers, was shot seven times in the back while removing his computer from his car's trunk (he survived). A tavern owner who refused to sell drugs for the HAMC was beaten to death on his front lawn. However, Boucher's reign of terror was coming to an end.

The Canadian Court of Appeals ordered a new trial, as requested by the prosecution. This is not considered double jeopardy in Canada. The court ruled that the trial judge erred in his charge to the jury. No insignias or colors were allowed at the new trial. In May 2002, Boucher was found guilty of the murder of two prison guard members and the attempted murder of a third. He was sentenced to life in prison. Under his reign, however, the deadliest organized crime war in history took place, with 160 dead—and 12 of them, like Daniel Desrochers, only guilty of being "in the wrong place at the wrong time."

Bandidos MC

Donald Eugene Chambers

Donald Eugene Chambers was founder and first "El Presidente" of the Bandidos MC. It is unknown how many people Chambers ordered to be killed, or killed himself, but Chambers was sent to prison for the execution murders of two brothers who sold him "bad dope." Biker legend proclaims the Bandidos MC (actually called the Bandidos Motorcycle *Gang*) was founded by Chambers when the disillusioned U.S. Marine returned from combat service in Vietnam (Hayes, 2011; www.onepercenterbikers.com). However, Ed Winterhalder, a former Bandidos leader and prolific writer on outlaw bikers, offers another version of the group's founding. Winterhalder and De Clercq (2008) accept that Chambers is a former Marine but state that Chambers was anything but a disillusioned Vietnam vet. They say,

> The closest he got to Vietnam was watching the news. Whether he was disillusioned or not is a moot point; it sounds good in print and gels with the clichéd portrayal of bikers. In society's collective consciousness, anybody who starts or joins an outlaw motorcycle club must be disillusioned, disturbed, antisocial, or rebelling against something—perhaps all of the above.
>
> *(2008: xiv; personal communication)*

In an earlier work, this author (Barker, 2015a) also debunks the disillusioned veteran myth and its effect on joining Outlaw Motorcycle Gangs, contending that the majority of those who join the Bandidos or other OMC/Gs, then and now, are thugs, bullies, and criminals with arrest records.

Chambers was convicted and sentenced to life in prison for a drug-related double homicide in 1972. As would become routine in following years when prosecuting Outlaw Motorcycle Gangs, a Bandidos prospective member who participated in the murders "ratted out" the killers. The informant contacted the FBI office and gave them the details. Biker claims of a close-knit "brotherhood" seem to be more rhetoric than reality (*Chambers* v. *State*, 1974). Court documents reveal Chambers and two other Bandidos members kidnapped two drug dealers from El Paso, Texas (one was 22 years old and the other 17), who had ripped them off in a drug deal. The two men sold a Bandidos member "speed" for $1,000 that turned out be baking powder. The two men were tortured for several hours and then were driven out into the desert, forced to dig their graves, and shot to death.

Ronnie Hodge took over as Bandidos El Presidente after Chambers's conviction. Hodge expanded the criminal and violent activities of the Bandidos (Barker, 2015a) by forging links with Colombian drug dealers who supplied the Bandidos with cocaine and perfected the manufacturing of high-quality methamphetamine. Chambers was paroled in 1983, retired from the gang, and was not known to be involved in Bandidos activities after that. He died of cancer in 1999.

The current national president, national vice-president, and national sergeant at arms have been indicted and accused of directing, sanctioning, approving, and permitting other members of the Bandidos to carry out racketeering acts including murder, attempted murder, assault, intimidation, extortion, and drug trafficking for the criminal organization (U.S. Department of Justice, January 6, 2016). In 2013, the Bandidos leadership declared war against the Cossacks MC, resulting in the

2015 carnage in Waco, Texas, which will be discussed in Chapter 8. One of the men charged in the current indictment has already pleaded guilty to a 2002 murder allegedly directed and sanctioned by the Bandidos leadership. It appears that one or more of the other national officers has agreed to testify against the national president for leniency. So much for brotherhood and the biker code of omertà.

Outlaws MC

Harry "Taco" Bowman

Harry "Taco" Bowman's long reign as the International Outlaws President is marked by extreme violence and cooperation with organized crime groups such as the Mafia. He served as an Outlaws regional president and national vice-president before becoming international president in 1984. As international president, Bowman set policies and directed the actions of Outlaws members and monitored members' activities in all chapters. He lived the life of an influential crime boss, residing in an affluent Detroit suburb, sending his children to private schools, and driving an armor-plated Cadillac, all the while making decisions on who would die or be beaten in his gang or in rival gangs. He was, in a word, a ruthless violent despot feared by all in the biker world because of his mercurial temper and violence.

Bowman's leadership came to an end in 1997 with his indictment for three murders and bombings. He fled the court's jurisdiction and remained on the run and on the FBI's Most Wanted List until his capture in 1999. His brutal reign of terror is documented in his 2002 appeal (*United States v. Bowman*, 2002).

In 1984, Bowman learned that a former Florida Outlaws MC member was planning to reveal the whereabouts of a fugitive member of the Outlaws. In response, Bowman directed his trusted right-hand man, Wayne "Joe Black" Hicks, to go to Florida, find the former Outlaw, and kill him.

(In an interesting aside, it was Hicks who would be the main witness at Bowman's trial 15 years later, once again demonstrating outlaw biker Brotherhood is more rhetoric than reality. Hicks saved himself from a long prison sentence by "ratting out" his friend and mentor, supporting the saying that "the first rat gets the best deal" (see Box 6.1). Both police and prosecutors know that outlaw bikers and crooked cops, who both claim to be "brothers," can flip like acrobats when confronted with long prison sentences or the death penalty.)

Hicks was unable to find the former Outlaws member, but Bowman transferred him to Florida to revive the failing Fort Lauderdale chapter. Hicks later became that chapter's president and later a regional president.

Hicks reported to Bowman that a Florida Outlaws member had testified before a grand jury, which is a serious breach of conduct in an outlaw biker culture in which cooperation with authorities is considered "snitching." Bowman ordered Hicks to kick the errant member out of the club and "take care of him." Hicks and another Outlaw "pulled the snitch's patch" and administered a severe beating. The next violent act resulted in a former Outlaw's brutal murder.

In the 1990s, the Florida Warlocks MC aligned themselves with the Outlaws' hated rivals, the Hells Angels, and began selling drugs in territory claimed by the Outlaws. This alliance ignited a war between the Outlaws and the Hells Angels. Bowman then found out that a former Outlaw,

BOX 6.1 A REAL GOOD OUTLAW—WAYNE "JOE BLACK" HICKS

"I have no problem breaking [the] law," "Joe Black" Hicks answered. "I was an Outlaw, that was the least of my concerns. I was a good Outlaw" (Chachere, March 29, 2001).

Hicks was a good Outlaw. No one disputes that. As a good outlaw and Taco Bowman's right-hand man, he may have been responsible for as many as 20 murders in carrying out orders of the vicious Bowman (Sallah, June 3, 2001). Hicks committed his first murder in 1978 when he found himself on the losing end of a fight and stabbed his opponent in the jugular vein in Toledo, Ohio. He went on the run to Dayton, Ohio, and stayed with the Outlaws. Two months later, he surrendered, and plea bargained to a voluntary manslaughter charge and was sentenced to five to 25 years in prison. In the 1980s, he met Taco Bowman, the National President of the Outlaws. His career as the main Outlaws enforcer began.

Raymond "Bear" Chaffin, was the leader of the Warlocks' Edgewater, Florida, chapter. Bowman ordered Hicks to kill Bear Chaffin. Hicks then told an Outlaws prospect that if he killed Chaffin he would become a full-patched member and receive the Nazi SS-style lightning bolt patch for killing for the club. The prospect agreed; he approached Chaffin from behind in his garage and shot him four times in the head. The killer received his patch and the lightning bolts.

In March 1992, an Outlaws prospect violated a strict Outlaws rule at the Daytona Bike Week by getting into an altercation with an Outlaws leader and striking him. The prospect was brought to Bowman's hotel room and Bowman punched him in the face and put a knife to his throat; he was told to never strike another Outlaws member. Bowman instructed the other three Outlaws in the room to beat the prospect and get rid of him. They beat and kicked the man, and then pushed him off the third-story balcony. He lived, but had severe injuries, including a broken ankle. The former prospect considered himself lucky and refused to give any details to the police.

In 1994, Bowman, as the Outlaws International President, complained to the Chicago chapter president about the presence of the Hells Henchmen MC, an HAMC ally, in Chicago, and told him to get rid of them. Several bombings took place at the Hells Henchmen's clubhouse, and then the clubhouse was doused in gasoline and burned to the ground. Bowman then turned his attention back to the Florida Warlocks MC.

Bowman directed the Florida Outlaws to get rid of the Florida Warlocks. A series of fire bombings of Warlocks clubhouses followed. More were planned, but a police raid of the Daytona Outlaws broke up the plot and seized the firebombs. The next violent incident clearly demonstrates the mercurial nature of Bowman's temper and need for revenge.

The Fifth Chapter Motorcycle Club (FCMC) is a conventional family-oriented club composed of men and women recovering from substance abuse problems. Members consider themselves to be neutral and not aligned with any Outlaw Motorcycle Club or Gang. However, that did not protect them from Bowman's wrath when he determined that they disrespected him and the Outlaws. At the funeral of a Hells Angels member, who was killed in an altercation with an Outlaws member in 1984, a Fifth Chapter member was photographed hugging an Angel in comfort. Bowman considered this disrespectful to the Outlaws and ordered the FCMC to be disbanded and its members punished. The FCMC was invited to a party at the Orlando Outlaws chapter. When they arrived, they were seated at two picnic tables and surrounded by armed Outlaws. The Outlaws told them they were no longer allowed to exist as a motorcycle club and ordered them to remove all logos and FCMC insignias. The FCMC men and women were severely beaten and told to leave without congregating or going to the hospital. The Fifth Chapter Motorcycle Club ceased to exist.

Acts of internecine violence for control purposes have been recorded as well. At one time, Bowman suspected an Outlaws member was a snitch and planned his murder. Bowman told Hicks that the member should be killed and to make it look like an enemy did it. The man was then to receive an elaborate Outlaws funeral to hide the real motive. The member was shot in the head and dumped in a field next to the Outlaws clubhouse. The Outlaws spread the rumor that a cop who had been interested in the deceased Outlaw's girlfriend had killed him. All was forgotten, and no revenge was sought (a dead giveaway that the murder story was suspect).

In 1999, Bowman was convicted of racketeering, conspiracy to commit murder, and various drug and firearms offenses. He was sentenced to life in prison without parole. Bowman's life of crime, violence, and using and selling drugs was over, but the OMC/G's legacy of violence continued. One other Outlaws member escaped prosecution for crimes ordered by Bowman. In 1997, Outlaws leader, Regional President Randy "Mad Dog" Yager, fled prosecution and was captured in Mexico in 2014. See Figure 6.1.

Randy "Mad Dog" Yager

Randy "Mad Dog" Yager was the Outlaws regional president of the Chicago Region and president of the Gary, Indiana, Outlaws MC chapter. His regional duties covered Illinois, Indiana, and Wisconsin at the time when Harry "Taco" Bowman was the Outlaws International President and Wayne "Joe Black" Hicks was the national vice-president. As regional president, he put into action the ordered attacks on the Outlaws enemies, the Hells Henchmen in Chicago. A deputy U.S. Marshal described him as a vicious man, saying, "A lot of the [other Outlaws members] were scared [of him] because they thought he was crazy" (Macedo, November 24, 2008).

Yager was implicated in the bombing of the Hells Henchmen clubhouse and several vehicles, as well as the murders of an elderly couple in northern Illinois. He was part of a conspiracy to kill rival Hells Angels members, too. In 1997, Yager was one of 17 Outlaws members to be indicted in a massive racketeering case that involved murder, arson, and the use of explosives (Macedo, November 24, 2008). The other 16 defendants were immediately arrested, charged, and convicted of numerous crimes, but not Yager. He was in Las Vegas with his girlfriend when the raids and arrests were made. He fled, and Yager was put on the ATF's 15 Most Wanted List. Seventeen years later he was found in Rosarito, Mexico.

Rosarito, Mexico, is described as a sleepy tight-knit community of American expatriates and retirees, 20 miles south of the U.S.–Mexico border (Trimble, October 25, 2014). Steve and Margie Rothman, as they were known, lived in the town for over a decade and made their living doing odd jobs and house watching. Steve Rothman was looked on as a "nice oddball." Oddball because in an area where people dressed in shorts, tee shirts, and sandals, he wore work boots and denim coveralls over long-sleeved flannel shirts. This was all in an attempt to hide his neo-Nazi and biker tattoos.

MOST WANTED

Name: Randy Mark YAGER

Alias: Randy Michael YAGER, Randy WISLOCKA, "Mad"

Description:

Sex: . . . . MALE

Race: . . . . WHITE

Date of Birth: . . . . AUGUST 7, 1956

Place of Birth: . . . . INDIANA

Height: . . . . 5'11"

Weight: . . . . 235 POUNDS

Eyes: . . . . HAZEL

Hair: . . . . BROWN

Scars/Tattoos: . . . . TATTOOS LEFT ARM:

                 HARLEY DAVIDSON LOGO

                 OUTLAW INDIANS

                 TATTOO RIGHT ARM: EAGLE

                 SCAR: ABDOMEN

Wanted For: . . . . .Racketeering, including murder, firearms & explosives, arson, narcotics trafficking

Warrant Issued: . . . . . . .Eastern District of Wisconsin

Warrant Number: W019756852

Date of Warrant: . . . . . . .August 6, 1997

ARMED AND DANGEROUS – KNOWN TO CARRY MULTIPLE FIREARMS

YAGER is a member of the violent "Outlaws" motorcycle gang. The federal RICO charges include multiple charges of murder, firearms and explosives violations, arson, robbery, counterfeiting U.S. currency, trafficking in stolen vehicles and narcotics. YAGER usually wears a mustache, goatee or beard.

NOTICE: Before arrest, verify warrant through the National Crime Information Center (NCIC). If arrested or whereabouts known contact the nearest United States Marshals Service office or call the United States Marshals Service Headquarters at **1 (800) 336-0102.**

For more information see the U.S. Marshals Service website www.usmarshals.gov

FIGURE 6.1 "Wanted Poster" for Randy Mark Yager.

Source: Courtesy of U.S. Department of Justice, United States Marshals Service.

Steve and Margie were in a bar, eating steak and drinking beer, when the Mexican police, acting on a tip from the U.S. Marshals, confronted them. "Steve" (Yager) had false identification, but eventually confessed his true identity. "Margie" was allowed to leave the bar. She left the scene in a hurry, pursued by Mexican authorities wanting to search the vehicle. She flipped the car three times and then shot herself in the head as the officers approached. Yager was returned to the United States for trial. In March 2016, he agreed to a plea and sentencing agreement, which is sealed (*The Aging Rebel*, April 5, 2016).

The line of Outlaws National Presidents' involvement in crime and violence has continued. Bowman's successor, James "Frank" Wheeler, took over in 2001. Three years later, he was convicted of racketeering, conspiracy to commit racketeering, and conspiracy to distribute drugs. He is sentenced to life in prison. Jack "Milwaukee Jack" Rosga assumed the Outlaws national leadership when Wheeler was convicted. In 2010, Rosga was convicted of conspiring to engage in racketeering activities and conspiring to commit violence in aid of racketeering (U.S. Department of Justice, December 21, 2010). He is sentenced to 20 years in prison.

Devils Diciples

The Devils Diciples MC (DDMC) national president, national vice-president, and national warlord were convicted of participating in violent acts in aid of racketeering, methamphetamine production and trafficking, illegal firearms offenses, obstruction of justice, illegal gambling, and other federal offenses (U.S. Department of Justice, February 20, 2015). The national headquarters of the Diciples (which is intentionally misspelled) is in Clinton Township, Michigan, with regional chapters in Alabama, Arizona, California, Indiana, and Ohio.

Court testimony reveals numerous internecine acts of violence as control techniques to enforce club rules. The national president and national vice-president shot and killed a DDMC member in 2007 who had disobeyed gang rules. The national president attacked the girlfriend of a member because he believed she had disrespected him.

Devils Diciples members robbed, kidnapped, and attempted to murder Arizona chapter members in 2003 at the direction of the national leadership for rule violations. The members were taken to the clubhouse, bound with duct tape and zip ties, and severely beaten. The victims were then loaded into the bed of a pickup truck, driven into the desert, dumped into ravines, and left to die. The national president told one of the participants in a letter that the Devils Diciples were "all proud of them."

In 2012, DDMC members in Michigan encountered a rival outlaw biker present in DDMC territory without permission. He was knocked unconscious and suffered multiple fractures to his face and jaw. The DDMC members ripped his vest and colors off and left him lying in the street.

Phantom's MC

The predominately black Phantom's MC is an example of an OMC/G operating as a violent criminal organization. Antonio Johnson, aka "Mister Tony," "MT," and "Big Bro," is the National President of the Phantom's and the "Three-Star General" of the Michigan Vice Lords street gang, a national violent organized criminal street gang (U.S. Department of Justice, March

16, 2015). The connection between OMGs and criminal street gangs is increasing, but this is the only example this author is aware of in which dual membership has been found. Antonio Johnson and Marvin Nicholson, the Phantom's National Enforcer—also a Vice Lords member—were convicted of engaging in a RICO conspiracy, that is, conspiracy to commit murder in aid of racketeering, assault with a dangerous weapon in aid of racketeering, conspiracy to assault with a dangerous weapon in aid of racketeering, using and carrying firearms during and in relation to a crime of violence, and being a felon in possession of firearms.

The Phantom's MC headquarters is in Detroit and has chapters in Michigan, Ohio, Kentucky, Illinois, New York, New Jersey, Texas, Georgia, Missouri, and Tennessee, as well as a Nomads chapter that travels nationally. The Phantom's leadership used Vice Lords members in criminal enterprises and to search for and violently attack rival OMC/G members.

Kingsmen MC

Multiple leaders of the Kingsmen MC, including the national president and regional and chapter presidents, were among the 16 officers and members indicted in a major racketeering operation in New York (U.S. Department of Justice, March 22, 2016). One chapter president pleaded guilty and admitted that the Kingsmen MC (KMC) was a criminal organization engaging in drug distribution, firearms sales, committing violence, and promoting prostitution. The violent acts committed included the following:

- The national president ordered the murder of two KMC members who broke KMC rules (internecine violence for control purposes).
- A KMC leader shut down a chapter and took the members' "colors" for rule violations. They struck one member in the head and used bleach to clean up the blood. One of the chapter presidents was elevated to Nomads status for his role in the "patch pulling."
- A chapter president was involved in a drive-by shooting of a former member's residence because he had assaulted a KMC regional president.
- A female victim was repeatedly punched in the face by a KMC member and then held in the clubhouse for two days to conceal her facial injuries.

As shown above, joining an OMC/G or a street gang increases the chances of being a violence victim, either from fellow gang members or rivals.

7

VIOLENT PUBLIC EVENTS AND BIKER WARS

Events that Trigger Moral Panic

Introduction

OMC/G violence is most dangerous when it exposes innocent citizens to injury and death. These instances serve as the most likely triggering events of a "moral panic," which occurs when spontaneous, impulsive violence and planned aggressive violence—biker wars large and small—take place in public spaces. Historically, the largest number of planned aggressive violent incidents occurred in private, remote settings or routine spaces in the saloon society such as bars, tattoo shops, or other biker hangouts. However, they also occur in public settings, which greatly increases public attention and the likelihood of government action.

This inquiry is bracketed by two such violent events in U.S. public spaces: Altamont, California, Speedway on December 6, 1969—an example of spontaneous, impulsive violence fueled by alcohol and other drugs—and the massacre at Waco, Texas, on May 17, 2015—an example of planned aggressive violence exacerbated by police action. Both events occurred in public places, put innocent victims at risk, and received sensational media coverage. The events, 46 years apart, shocked the world and focused attention on the brutality associated with outlaw bikers as the public was reminded of how they assault, maim, and kill rivals, one another, and innocents. The massacre at Waco is worthy of inquiry because of the number of victims killed and injured by police action and the disastrous social effects on innocent people by the authorities' knee-jerk overreaction.

Planned Aggressive Violence: Biker Wars Large and Small

Quinn and Forsyth (2011) opine that the increasing elitism of the Hells Angels MC and their expansion across North America, Australia, and Europe since the 1990s reduced the number of planned aggressive acts between individual small OMCs. However, the expansion increased the likelihood of planned aggressive acts by large OMC/Gs, such as the Outlaws, Bandidos, Mongols, Vagos, Pagans, and others, in North America, as well as U.S.-based and indigenous OMCs outside the continental United States—particularly those most interested in power and profit. In the middle to late 1960s, a new orientation swept through the outlaw biker world as violent criminals emerged as leaders and the clubs became involved in drug trafficking. Quinn and Forsyth believe that post-1990 OMC/Gs are driven by the rational goal of profit through organized crime and use planned aggressive violence as a tool to achieve that goal. The planned aggressive violence to achieve rational goals is reflected in the number, intensity, frequency, and viciousness of the wars between OMCs and the HAMC and its affiliates. Biker wars, including internecine wars, continue in the OMC/G world, as we see in the recounting that follows. Planned aggressive violence increases the likelihood of more violence.

Biker wars increase criminal activities and recruitment of violence-prone members. Outlaw bikers at war concentrate on the "specific missions" and how to pay for them (Quinn and Forsythe, 2011). Wars are expensive—members give up legitimate work activities to fight and defend, weapons and explosives are purchased, clubhouses are fortified, and legal expenses are paid. Therefore, member's dues and fees go up, increasing the likelihood of organized criminal behavior to support the war effort. Often, membership requirements are relaxed and prospect periods are reduced to recruit known violent "warfighters" and lesser qualified members to become "cannon fodder." Many of those recruited would not be allowed to join in peacetime.

Before we examine examples of planned aggressive violence acts, we recount the spontaneous impulsive violence that occurred at the Altamont, California, Speedway in December of 1969. This single event put outlaw biker violence on display for the world and earned worldwide infamy for the Hells Angels Motorcycle Club (HAMC) (Barker, 2015a), revealing them to be very dangerous (Morton, 1999). Ever since, outlaw bikers have been recognized as violent threats to anyone who came into contact with them.

Spontaneous Impulsive Biker Violence in Public Settings

Altamont Speedway, December 1969: Hells Angels Motorcycle Club Earns Worldwide Infamy

"Out-of-control disaster" is an appropriate descriptor of what took place on a cold Saturday, December 6, 1969, at Altamont Speedway, which was in a remote location on the southern edge of Alameda County, California. Some call the events that took place at a free concert that day the most violent day in rock music history (Barker, 2015a).

In the middle of nowhere, the Speedway could only be accessed by a single four-lane highway, which would soon become clogged. Three hundred thousand young concert fans, many under the influence of drugs, rode, walked, and stumbled to the location. They witnessed a series of tragic events, which many contend to have been set in motion by the bad judgment and avarice of Mick Jagger of the rock group, The Rolling Stones, and the band's sycophants (Selvin, 2016). According to Selvin, if Jagger had not insisted on keeping all the money from the documentary that was made, the "free concert" would have been held at the Sears Point Raceway outside of San Francisco. The Sears Point Raceway had ample parking, toilets, concession stands, water, and electricity. Security was already there, and the police were nearby if needed. All these amenities were absent at Altamont and probably would have prevented the catastrophe that occurred, as the Hells Angels would not have been in charge. A stage could have been set up inside the Sears Point track to provide a natural barrier between the audience and the performers, but at Altamont the stage was four feet high with a small white cord around the top, giving easy access to the stage and the performers by rambunctious and intoxicated fans. Fans could and did easily step up on stage, eliciting violent reactions by out-of-control Hells Angels. (In contrast, earlier that year, the stage at the Woodstock, a music festival near Woodstock, New York, that famously attracted an audience of more than 400,000, was 15 feet high.) By the end of the concert, there were four deaths—one drowning, two automobile crash deaths, and a "racially motivated" murder that was caught on film—along with multiple injuries suffered by performers, journalists, and concert fans by out-of-control and drug-fueled Hells Angels.

The planning for the Altamont concert began in London and spiraled out of control as the guiding hand of The Grateful Dead ("the Dead") was countermanded by Mick Jagger. According to Selvin, in the fall of 1969, Rock Sully, the manager of the San Francisco rock band The Grateful Dead arrived in London to meet with The Rolling Stones (the "Stones") to convince them to go on an American tour, culminating in a free concert in San Francisco. The Stones were receptive. Their high-living lifestyle had left them broke, with more debts than assets. An American tour would replenish their coffers and meet the challenge to their celebrity from The Beatles and the recent Woodstock concert (Selvin, 2016). Free outdoor concerts had been the norm in San Francisco since the advent of the Haight-Ashbury counterculture. The enormous Golden Gate Park would be natural venue for such an event.

According to Selvin, Jagger's hatred for the police was a huge factor in the Hells Angels providing security at the Altamont concert (Selvin, 2016). Jagger had witnessed and experienced the heavy-handed actions of the European police as they used tear gas, batons, dogs, and water cannons on unruly audiences, even having had his arm broken in one of these melees. Before the U.S. tour started, Jagger insisted that no uniformed police officers would be allowed at any Stones concert (Selvin, 2016). It was written into the contracts. He would live to regret that stipulation. At the London meeting, the Dead's manager Sully told Jagger that assuring no police would be no problem; the Hells Angels had handled security at the Haight-Ashbury free concerts. "The Angels are really some righteous dudes," he said, "They carry themselves with honor and dignity" (Selvin, 2016: 70). In general, the California Haight-Ashbury hippies accepted the bikers as fellow rebels against straight society. However, this was going to be different.

Jagger and his entourage readily accepted the idea of the Hells Angels as security. The London Hells Angels had been used at English concerts without problems. The London Hells Angels who guarded the stage at Hyde Park concerts, however, were considered a "candy-ass" imitation of the California "real deal" Angels. The Hyde Park Hells Angels rode around on mopeds wearing cleanly polished leathers with motorcycle jackets with Hells Angels drawn in white chalk on the back (Selvin, 2016). The California Hells Angels were not the same.

At the first meeting about the security arrangement, the California Hells Angels representative made it clear. "We ain't no cops," he said. Sam Cutler, the English tour manager, assured the Hell Angels that they would not have to act as cops; the Stones would have their own security. The Hells Angels would be retained to keep people off the stage, give people directions, and keep civilians out of the backstage area. The deal was struck for $500 in beer. It can be said that the Stones certainly got their money's worth. The Hell Angels kept people off the stage and out of the backstage area. It was *how* they earned their $500 in beer that was the problem.

On the day of the concert, Hells Angels members from the San Francisco chapter arrived early and started partying, drinking cheap red wine and doing other drugs. The majority of them were prospects and junior members. The chapter's officers were at an HAMC officers meeting in Oakland with Sonny Barger, leaving the partying Angels without any real supervision. As previously noted, "prospects" can be particularly dangerous because many are real bullies who have not been "culled out" yet, and they are under scrutiny by full-patched members looking for evidence of class. The prospects wanted to show off just how bad they could be. One prospect, puffed up by his Hells Angels status, passed through the crowd snatching wine from the fans and taking it back to impress his "brothers." Making things potentially worse, the bikers parked their bikes in front of the stage. Stoned and drunk fans crowded around the bikes, creating a volatile situation. Under these dangerous conditions, the concert got under way.

The band Santana kicked the concert off around 1:00 PM, and the Hells Angels' first victim, a naked, overweight man, apparently high on something, started his way to the stage. The Angels, largely San Jose Hells Angels members and prospects, began beating him unmercifully. A Grateful Dead associate familiar with many of the San Francisco Angels jumped off the stage and begged the offending Angels to stop the attack. Strangely, they did. As the victim started to leave, however, he turned and punched a Hells Angels member before quickly disappearing into the crowd. The Angels, now angered, then turned on the Dead associate and began pummeling him with pool cues, leaving their severely beaten victim lying in front of the stage. The beaten man was taken backstage to an improvised medical center, where it took 60 stitches to close the wounds on his head and face.

The LSD guru Timothy Leary was backstage and asked to take the stage and calm things down. He responded, "These people [Hells Angels] are crazy and out of control" (Selvin, 2016: 165). Santana played for 45 minutes, and the Angels went into the crowd at least six more times swinging their pool cues. The Hells Angels chased a photographer in front of the stage, beating him because he would not give up the film from his camera. While all of this was going on, some San Francisco Hells Angels, standing on top of a bus that brought them to the concert, began throwing full beer cans at the stage, knocking those they hit unconscious. Selvin (2016) reports the San Jose members turned on a prospect for some reason and beat him senseless. As soon as he recovered, he rejoined his "brothers."

Jefferson Airplane was the next group to take the stage, as the Angels sat on the edge of the stage drinking beer. Fans were sitting on the stage with them. Then the Angels started fighting with fans in front of the stage, and Jefferson Airplane vocalist Marty Balin intervened. The Angels were beating a black man, and Balin yelled at them to stop. He threw his tambourine at the Angels and began yelling at an Angels member called "Animal." Animal smashed Balin in the face, knocking him down. Balin got up and jumped into the melee in front and was knocked unconscious by another Angel. Balin was taken backstage for medical treatment. Apparently feeling bad about beating a performer, Animal went backstage to apologize. That did not go well. Animal told Balin "You just can't say 'Fuck You' to an Angel." Balin stood up and yelled "Oh Yeah? Fuck you." Animal knocked him out again (Selvin, 2016: 177). A member of the Dead's road crew saw what had happened and confronted Animal. Animal knocked the man unconscious.

The Flying Burrito Brothers followed Jefferson Airplane, and at that point things calmed down somewhat. However, the Hells Angels found the first victim, the "naked fat man" who had punched the Angel before fading into the crowd. The Flying Burritos had hidden him in their trailer. Upon finding him, the Angels savagely beat him and knocked out his front teeth with pool cues. A naked woman who was walking around hugging people received the same reception he did.

When another group, Crosby, Stills, Nash, and Young (CSNY), reluctantly took the stage, the violence intensified. The Hells Angels attacked the surging crowd in front of the stage, and one Angel was seen pounding a stoned fan in the stomach while another Angel held him up. David Crosby pleaded with the crowd "Please stop hurting each other. You don't have to. You can always talk, man" (Selvin, 2016: 195). One Angel sat on the side of the stage with a sharpened motorcycle spoke and stabbed Stephen Stills in the leg every time he stepped forward to sing. When CSNY finished, Stills's legs and pants were soaked with blood.

As the monthly Officers Meeting of the Oakland Hells Angels was finishing, the officers in attendance were dealing with club business, unaware of what was happening at Altamont. Sonny Barger led the cadre of officers to Altamont and made a tragic error. Barger believed the first 40 feet in front of the stage had been cleared for them to park their bikes as a barrier between the stage and the crowd. When Barger got to the stage, he realized the trouble they were in and confided to another Angels member, called "Sweet William," "We're keeping this stage. Do you realize that if all these people had their minds together, they could crush this thing?" (Selvin, 2016: 2013). The Stones were in a nearby tent, killing time and tuning up to delay their entrance for dramatic effect. Barger sent Sweet William to hurry them up. According to Selvin (2016: 263), Sweet William relayed the message in blunt terms:

> "You better get the fuck out there before the place blows," he told Jagger. "You've tuned up enough." Jagger told them they were "preparing," and they would go on when they were ready. "I'm telling you," said Sweet William, "People are going to die out there. Get out there. You've been told." Succeeding events would show how prophetic Sweet William was.

When the Stones took the stage and started playing, Barger was standing on the stage and saw a fan "messing with" an Angels bike and smoke coming from it. Barger jumped off the stage, followed by his minions. Barger put out the fire, and the other Angels beat anyone within reach. The next incident was murder.

Meredith Hunter, an 18-year-old black man, attended the concert with a 17-year-old white girl and stood in the crowd in front of the stage. The girl would later testify that the Angels on stage gave them frequent menacing looks. Hunter, who had been taking speed, attempted to climb on stage. Angels pushed, threw him back, and began pounding him. Hunter pulled a gun from his waistband and stumbled sideways with the gun pointed at the ground. An Angel standing nearby saw the gun; he drew a knife from his boot and stabbed Hunter in the neck and back as the others kicked him in the head. The Angels would not allow anyone to aid Hunter as he lay on the ground bleeding out. Hunter was still alive when he reached the medical station, and the doctor said he needed immediate evacuation to a hospital, so he was rushed to a nearby helicopter. The pilot told the doctor the helicopter was reserved for the Stones and unavailable for medical emergencies (Selvin, 2016). An ambulance was called for, but Hunter was dead when it arrived.

The Hells Angels violence was not over. Several Hells Angels noticed a custom-made purple rug rolled up beside the stage and threw the rug on top of two Harleys in a pickup truck they were driving. Tour director Chip Monck saw them and explained the rug belonged to the Stones and it was his duty to return it. The Angels laughed and started driving off. Monck grabbed the rug and pulled it off, causing the two Harleys to fall and crash to the ground. The Angels beat him with pool cues and left him lying in the dirt with a broken nose and missing his front teeth.

San Francisco Hells Angel Alan Passaro, age 22, was eventually charged with stabbing Meredith Hunter five times. He was brought to trial in 1970. The film clip of the murder from the documentary was played for the jury several times. The jury found him not guilty. Passaro was found dead several years later, floating in a ravine under suspicious circumstances.

Planned Aggressive Violence: Selected Examples

The romantic view of the one-percenter would have us believe that they "live by a code that embodies courage, strength, pride, individualism and that does not tolerate humiliation" (*The Aging Rebel*, April 4, 2017). Spokesmen for the one-percenters proclaim that the "powerful brotherhoods that are the outlaw motorcycle clubs" are the epitome of this Brotherhood (Hayes, 2011: 6; Veno, 2009). However, the reality of outlaw biker life belies this romantic view. The question is: Why do bikers kill other brother bikers living the same lifestyle and following the same "code"? The answer seems to be that there is no real brotherhood among and between outlaw bikers. Constant planned aggressive violence has been a signal event in outlaw biker history since the 1950s as the brothers compete over territory, "showing class," and criminal markets. Altamont was not an aberration; it was just the first example of outlaw biker violence to receive worldwide publicity. The 1970s, 1980s, and 1990s were especially violent as one-percent outlaw clubs expanded throughout the United States and overseas.

1971: Hells Angels MC and the Breed MC

A battle between the Breed MC of Akron, Ohio, an offshoot of a New Jersey OMC/G, and members of the Cleveland Hells Angels, backed by members of the New York Hells Angels, at the fourth annual Motorcycle Custom and Trade show held at the Polish Women's Hall in Cleveland, Ohio, left five bikers (four Breed members and one NY Hells Angels member) dead, 20 injured, and 57 arrested (Anon. 8, March 8, 1971). There were three Cleveland police officers injured in the melee between warring outlaw bikers. The estimated 160 Breeds and 70 Angels and their supporters went after each other with knives, clubs, and chains. Members of both gangs say the others started the fight. Those arrested included 47 Breed members and 10 Hells Angels members. Fourteen Hells Angels would eventually plead guilty to manslaughter. The original newspaper report said the fight was between the Breed and the Violators, a chapter of the New York Hells Angels, but in truth the Violators were in the process of "patching over" to the Hells Angels. Jeffrey S. Coffey, a New York Hells Angels member, was killed in the brawl.

It appears that Nelson Blackburn, a Scottish immigrant and iron worker, formed the Cleveland, Ohio, Hells Angels chapter in December 1967, after a visit from Hells Angels leader Sonny Barger (Baird, November 5, 2011). The new Hells Angels chapter engaged in a series of wars with other Cleveland Outlaw Motorcycle Gangs, including the larger Breed MC, seeking to expand to Cleveland. In 1968, Blackburn and a dozen other Cleveland Angels got into an altercation with a black man in a bar on Cleveland's east side. The black man and one other man were killed. Blackburn ended up in prison, serving a 10-years-to-life sentence that was commuted to six years in 1975. He, along with other Cleveland Hells Angels, was in prison when the Breed MC attempted to drive the weakened Hells Angels out of Cleveland. Members of the New York Hells Angels chapter, including Jeffrey Coffey, were sent to Cleveland to bolster the fighting power of the local chapter. For example, J.C. Rogers, the leader of the Rochester, New York, chapter is listed on their website as having been one of the Hells Angels who went to Cleveland to fight the Breeds (www.hells-angels-rochester.com). The Middleton, Connecticut, Hells Angels chapter makes a yearly pilgrimage to Coffey's grave to pour whiskey over the grave (Hartford, June 18, 2002). The national Hells Angels were not about to let any other OMC/G drive one of the chapters out of Cleveland, especially a lesser club like the Breed MC.

The 22-year-old Hells Angels member Jeffery S. Coffey died the victim of a violent act; however, his funeral produced another violent act. Eight out-of-town Hells Angels attending his New York funeral were arrested and charged with forcible rape, sodomy, and unlawful imprisonment with a gang assault on a 17-year-old girl (Montgomery, March 12, 1971). The girl was beaten and raped for six hours while the owner of a leather shop was held captive. The Angels were in the leather shop purchasing items when they spotted the girl, the girlfriend of the owner, and began the sexual assault. The shop owner escaped and found police officers nearby. Finding the girl naked, incoherent, and suffering from shock, the police arrested the attackers in the shop. As the saying goes, "There are No Angels in the Hells Angels, that is why the Canadians call them the 'Hells.'"

1974: Biker War between HAMC and the Outlaws MC

As noted in Chapter 3, the HAMC began as an Outlaw Motorcycle Club and evolved into an Outlaw Motorcycle *Gang* under the leadership of Sonny Barger in the mid- to late 1960s. The Outlaws MC, established initially in 1935, evolved into an OMG in 1969, when the original Outlaws split into an outlaw club and a riding club. Famed photojournalist Danny Lyons joined the Outlaws MC in 1965 and produced the first photo documentary on outlaw bikers, first published in 1968 (Lyons, 2003). His classic work documents that the Hells Angels and the Outlaws were not always enemies. One picture in the photodocumentary shows a Hells Angels member in full colors riding on the same bike behind an Outlaws member wearing his colors (Barker, 2007). Enmity between the two groups began with the HAMC expansion and the competition over drug markets. Power and profit became more important than any former sense of brotherhood. One triggering event became the impetus for the Hells Angels to declare war on all Outlaws MC members—a situation that still exists and shows no indication of ever ending.

According to George Christie, media celebrity and former Hells Angels national leader, the bloody war between the Hells Angels and the Outlaws MC had its beginning in a dispute over the treatment of a woman (Christie, 2016). In 1969, Sandy Alexander, who would later become a legendary HAMC leader, visited the Oakland, California, Hells Angels chapter to "patch over" his New York Aliens MC to the Hells Angels. While Alexander was in California, Frank "Greased Lightning" Rogers, a member of the Aliens MC, "took liberties" with Alexander's wife and left before Alexander returned. Rogers fled to Florida and joined the Outlaws MC. When Rogers returned to New York to visit friends in 1974, Alexander, a martial arts expert, learned of his return, tracked him down, and beat him almost to death. Rogers returned to Florida and told his Outlaws brothers that he had been "rat-packed" by the New York Hells Angels. This would show disrespect to the Outlaws MC, setting in motion the events that followed.

Two Massachusetts Hells Angels rode to Florida to make sure that a former member who was kicked out of the Lowell, Massachusetts, chapter for stealing club money had removed his club tattoo and returned all HAMC gear. They did not wear their "colors," which would have been a sign of disrespect. He was unaware of the tale that Rogers had told of being "rat-packed" by Hells Angels and that the Outlaws were seeking revenge. The Hells Angels viewed the earlier event as a personal beef between two outlaw bikers, and their current assignment was a routine "surrendering" of club material and "blacking out tattoos" that takes place when a member leaves a club. The Outlaws, on the other hand, saw an opportunity to retaliate for the "rat-pack" beating and supposed disrespect of an Outlaws member. Learning that the Hells Angels were in town, the Outlaws members invited the HAMC members over to their clubhouse, ostensibly for friendly drinks. Following a drinking session, their new "friends" proclaimed that no decent Outlaws member would drink with "scum" Hells Angels (Lavigne, 1999). The situation turned deadly. The Outlaws beat the HAMC members, tied them up, and took them to a flooded quarry. Standing the two Angels on the bank facing the water, the Outlaws tied concrete blocks to their feet and executed them with shotguns (Christie, 2016). The Hells Angels–Outlaws war was on.

1975: Biker War in New Zealand

A war between the indigenous New Zealand Highway 61 MC and the encroaching U.S.-based Hells Angels resulted in the death of a Highway 61 officer and nine Hells Angels convicted and sentenced (Gilbert, 2013). The war began with a firebombing of a Hells Angels rental property and a nighttime retaliation raid on the Highway 61's clubhouse by masked Hells Angels. A Highway 61 member lying on the floor was shot in the head by a shotgun. The defense claimed the shotgun discharged accidentally; they said the HA members had carried it in only to scare the rival club members. Following a four-week trial, nine Hells Angels members were convicted of manslaughter and sentenced to between seven and 10 years of incarceration. There is still bad blood between the two Outlaw Motorcycle Gangs today. However, the tension now is over criminal markets and power.

1977: Hells Angels MC Declares War on the Mongols MC

There are several accounts of what started the war between the Mongols and the Hells Angels in 1977. However, to this author's knowledge, there is only one account by someone who was a California Hells Angels member at the time and was a member of the "hit teams" looking for Mongols to kill. George Christie, the former member of the Hells Angels Ventura chapter, described the events leading up to and during the war in his autobiography, *Exile on Front Street: My Life as a Hell Angels and Beyond* (Christie, 2016). Christie prospected with the Hells Angels in 1975 and became a full-patched member in 1976. He founded the Ventura chapter and served as its president for more than 30 years.

Christie writes that, contrary to popular belief, the precipitating event to the Mongols-versus-Hells Angels war began in March 1977 at a Southern California motorcycle swap meet in what he called a "stupid fight" over a woman. A former Richmond Hells Angels member, Bud Green, was kicked out of the club for testifying against a fellow Angel in a murder trial. Green joined the Mongols and was living with the ex-wife of a Los Angeles Hells Angel. When nine Angels members, including Christie, walked into the swap meet, the Mongols and Bud Green greeted and surrounded them. In the Hells Angels contingency was the cuckolded Hells Angels member, and the brawl started immediately.

The outnumbered Angels held their own and seriously injured a number of Mongols before the police arrived. As Christie describes it, a skinny young cop with a buzz cut and a sharply pressed sheriff's uniform stood in the middle of the fighting bikers, pulled his pistol, and told everyone to stop fighting. The stunned bikers ceased bashing each other and tried to flee. The Angels ran to the exit and escaped, leaving the Mongols to be arrested by the arriving back-up officers. The agitated and disrespected Angels returned to their clubhouse and contemplated their next move against the Mongols, who had the temerity to disrespect the Hells Angels. The Hells Angels' basic code—"If you throw down with any Hells Angels, you throw down with all Hells Angels"—had been breached (Christie, 2016: 60), and the war was on.

Then, the Los Angeles Hells Angels chapter president made an ill-advised truce with the Mongols at a time when the rest of the Hells Angels, including Sonny Barger's Oakland Chapter, were bent on retaliation. He was forced to resign, and the situation got worse. The new president was a meth addict who soon got himself into deep trouble. He recorded a conversation with the Mongols leader that revealed his weakness and the brazenness of the Mongols (Christie, 2016: 63). The Mongols' leader said, "Hey, we've been doing a lot of thinking and we're going to a California rocker." The response was, "Maybe you could go to a Golden State rocker?" to which the Mongols leader laughingly replied, "No, we're pretty set on a California rocker."

The Los Angeles Hells Angels chapter president presented the recorded conversation at a West Coast Hells Angels Officers meeting. The stunned officers could not believe a Hells Angels officer would tolerate such disrespect or that the Mongols would consider wearing the California bottom rocker without HAMC permission. The president and the Mongols were both in trouble; something would be done.

The majority of the Mongols were still displaying ("flying") local chapter bottom rockers, but reports were coming in that some were flying California rockers. Hells Angels hit teams were assigned to look for Mongols flying the California rocker. Christie and his heavily armed hit team searched but never found one. Then another Hells Angels hit team spotted a group of Mongols on a run on Interstate 15, just north of San Diego, flying the California rocker. All hell broke loose.

When one HAMC hit team, including the San Diego "Dago" chapter president, received word a pack of Mongols were heading their way on Interstate 15, they set up an ambush. The Angels were in a stolen car and armed with machine guns. They pulled up side-by-side with the lead riders. The Mongols president and his girlfriend were on one bike, and a Mongols member and his girlfriend were beside him. They were flying California bottom rockers. The Angels sprayed the lead riders with machine-gun fire, causing them to crash and setting off a chain reaction of crashing motorcycles with bikers and their passengers strewn all over the interstate. The lead Mongols riders were both dead at the scene. Their female passengers survived but were left paralyzed. Everyone in California now knew that the Hell Angels MC was at war with the Mongols MC. The two motorcycle clubs continue to kill each other to this day.

1980: Indigenous Biker War in Denmark

The U.S.-based Hells Angels made plans to establish a chapter in Denmark, creating a war between two indigenous motorcycle clubs, the Galloping Ghosts MC and the Bullshit MC, to see who would become the Hells Angels chapter (Barker, 2015a). Eight bikers were killed, and the Bullshit became the loser after its president was machine-gunned down. The typical pattern for Hells Angels expansion in Europe was to allow the competing gangs to fight it out, and the HAMC would take the winner (Sher and Marsden, 2006). They would use this tactic time and time again.

1983: Indigenous Biker War in England

In London, England, six members of the Road Rats MC and 24 members of the Satans Slaves MC, both homegrown motorcycle clubs but rivals, battled each other at an event sponsored by the Hells Angels (Barker, 2015a). The two rivals fought with guns, axes, knives, and baseball bats, leaving two Road Rats MC members dead.

1984: Milperra Massacre: Australia's Deadliest Biker War

Six bikers and a 14-year-old girl selling raffle tickets were killed in Milperra, Australia, a normally peaceful Sydney suburb, in the battle between the indigenous Comanchero MC and a recently formed U.S.-based Bandidos MC chapter (Barker, 2015a). The war in a public space—a parking lot of the only pub in the city—occurred on Australia's Fathers' Day. The rival gangs attacked each other with guns, knives, and baseball bats as innocent people scrambled for safety.

The animosity between the two groups arose over a drug-selling disagreement (Stephenson, 2004). The Australian Bandidos chapter members were originally Comanchero members who had chafed under the dictatorial leadership of William "Jock" Ross, the "supreme commander" of the Comanchero. Some members were particularly outraged at Ross's dictum against selling drugs. Ross was also accused of breaking one of his own rules, by having an affair with another member's wife.

The "breakaway" members contacted the Texas Bandidos and were granted membership, further driving a wedge between the two groups. Ross, who knew the newly created Bandidos would be at a swap meet in Milperra on Fathers' Day, ordered the Comanchero to attend in force and armed to confront their former "brothers." Forty-three bikers were charged with seven counts of murder. Ross received a life sentence and committed suicide in prison several years later. Seven other Comanchero received life sentences, and 16 Bandidos served 14 years for manslaughter. The two gangs are still bitter enemies.

1991: Pagans MC and Fates Assembly MC Biker War

The Pagans MC (founded in Prince George's County, Maryland, in 1959) and the Fates Assembly MC (founded in Anne Arundel County, Maryland, in 1974) were at times rivals in the Baltimore/Washington area. The tension between the two motorcycle clubs increased in the late 1980s and 1990s when the Fates Assembly became an ally of the Hells Angels MC; it increased to the point where the Fates Assembly declared war on the Pagans in 1991.

The first serious incident was a fight between the two groups on May 28, 1991, outside a Baltimore bar, resulting in the death of a Pagan and several injured Fates Assembly members (www.onepercenterbikers.com). A series of bombings and assassinations followed. An attempt to kill a Pagans member resulted in the death of a Fates Assembly member when the Pagans member returned fire. Fates Assembly then declared war on the Pagans, and the violence escalated. Fates

Assembly members threw a hand grenade into the residence of a Pagans member, but it failed to explode. Fates Assembly members also attempted several unsuccessful ambushes on the Pagans, raising the tension further between the gangs. A Fates Assembly member was later killed in a shootout with a Pagans member. The war ended when a Fates Assembly member turned government witness and testified against his former "brothers." The Fates Assembly national president and two chapter presidents were sent to prison, and the remaining members were then deemed worthy to "patch over" to the Hells Angels, thus dissolving the Fates Assembly MC.

1994: Outlaws MC and Hells Henchmen MC Biker War

This war was described in detail in Chapter 6 when discussing Harry "Taco" Bowman. Taco Bowman, the International President of the Outlaws MC, ordered that Outlaws members do something about the presence of the Hells Henchmen MC, an ally of the Hells Angels. The war was on, and bombings and shootings followed.

1994–1997: Great Nordic Biker War

During the Nordic Biker War, the Hells Angels MC and the Bandidos MC fought for control of the Scandinavian drug markets in Denmark, Sweden, Finland, and Norway, resulting in 11 murders, 74 attempted murders, and 96 wounded. There were more than 200 violent incidents. Although the number of deaths and injuries is high, given the violence and the armament of the gangs involved, it is remarkable that more were not killed and injured. The definitive work on the Hells Angels' European expansion and the violence it spawned is Sher and Marsden's seminal work, *Angels of Death: Inside the Biker Gangs' Crime Empire* (2006). In that book, the authors provide an in-depth analysis of the Great Nordic Biker War.

According to Sher and Marsden, the antecedents for the Great Nordic Biker were set in place when the HAMC decided to expand into Amsterdam in the Netherlands, which was considered the drug center of Europe in the 1970s. In 1977, an Amsterdam motorcycle club led by Willem van Boxtel petitioned to National and International HAMC president Sonny Barger for a Hells Angels charter. The club became a prospective Hells Angels chapter and was granted full-patch status in 1978. From this base, the Hells Angels began their expansion into Denmark, Sweden, Norway, and Finland. The HAMC was not the only U.S.-based outlaw biker gang interested in European expansion.

The Texas-based Bandidos, recognizing the potential drug trafficking market, moved to challenge the HAMC in Europe and share in the drug markets, sparking fears of an all-out biker war between these rivals all over the continent. According to Sher and Marsden (2006), representatives from both biker gangs recognized that a war between the two biker gangs would be "bad for business" and attempted to agree to a peace pact that would ensure "peaceful coexistence" and profit for all. They met in Paris to avert war and divide up Europe; the result was known as the Paris Peace Pact. However, the Bandidos realized they needed a base in Scandinavia to protect their interests and launch expansion at a later date, so they pushed the limits of the Paris Peace Pact. They patched over a small indigenous gang in Denmark and established two chapters in Denmark; their first move into Scandinavia. The Hells Angels agreed to the move if the Bandidos promised not to establish any more chapters in Scandinavia. The Bandidos agreed, but proceeded to increase expansion into Scandinavia. So much for a peace pact between criminal organizations who hate each other. The bloody wars common to the two biker gangs in the United States and Australia moved to Europe with a vengeance.

This war escalated slowly, with competing indigenous biker gangs in Copenhagen, Denmark, "patching over" to either the Hells Angels or the Bandidos and then declaring war on each other. The first death occurred on February 13, 1994, when armed Hells Angels members crashed a private party 15 Bandidos members were having at a club in Helsingborg, Sweden. When the shooting stopped, three bikers were wounded, and a Hells Angels "hangaround" was killed. In an extreme escalation, the two gangs brought heavy artillery into the war.

In Denmark and Sweden, the military has small-weapons depots located throughout the country for use by civilian militias in national defense. Military service is obligatory for all male citizens, so they know where these unguarded weapons depots are and they are trained in the use of the weapons. Hence, the biker gangs knew and took advantage of these heavy military weapons. The day after the shootout in Helsingborg, a weapons depot was broken into, and 16 shoulder-fired anti-tank weapons were stolen along with hundreds of hand grenades and crates of small arms, including pistols and military rifles, plus ammunition. It was not long before these weapons and other stolen armament began showing up in the hands of warring bikers in Sweden and Denmark.

The Swedish Hells Angels responded with carefully planned assassinations. On July 17, 1995, the Swedish Bandidos president was riding his Harley home on a deserted roadway near a thick forest when a concealed sniper shot him off his bike with an automatic rifle. The same day two Bandidos were killed outside their clubhouse in Helsinki, Finland, expanding the biker war. Within two weeks, the Bandidos launched two rocket attacks against Hells Angels clubhouses in Helsinki and Helsingborg. The attacks destroyed property, but no one was injured or killed. The war spread throughout Oslo and Copenhagen, as both biker gangs engaged in drive-by shootings and rocket attacks. The gangs fortified their clubhouses and lived in a constant state of siege. The next attack came in a public space—in broad daylight in front of hundreds of people.

On March 10, 1996, the Bandidos Danish leader, Uffe Larsen, and three gang members arrived at the Copenhagen, Denmark, airport on their way home from a Bandidos party in Helsinki, Finland. As they were getting in their car in the parking lot, a group of eight or 10 men approached the car, and two stepped forward and sprayed the car's windshield with machine-gun fire. Larsen was killed instantly and the others wounded. The same type of ambush was under way at the Fornebu Airport in Oslo, Norway, on Norwegian Bandidos returning from the same party. A Bandidos member was killed, and the four Angels involved in his murder received their "Filthy Few" patches (Sher and Marsden, 2006).

On April 11, 1996, rockets fired by Bandidos rained down on the Hells Angels clubhouses in Snoldelev, Denmark, near Copenhagen; the Hells Angels clubhouse outside of Helsingborg, Sweden; and an HAMC prospects' clubhouse in Jutland, Denmark. A week later, two anti-tank rockets were fired at two Hells Angels clubhouses in Copenhagen, burning one to the ground and killing an innocent woman. Then the Hells Angels retaliation occurred in Copenhagen—three in-prison attacks.

Hells Angels members cut through a perimeter fence at a Copenhagen prison, broke through a window, and threw a grenade under the bed of a sleeping Bandidos vice-president inmate. The grenade exploded, and the Hells Angels assassins machine-gunned the cell. The Bandidos vice-president was severely wounded but survived. The Angels then sent another imprisoned Bandidos member a shaver with a small bomb inside. The last prison attack occurred as a Hells Angels hit team walked into a low-security prison and threw a hand grenade into a cell.

The Bandidos retaliated in equally brazen form. Two weeks later, a Bandidos MC member climbed on top of a steeply slanted tiled roof that gave him clear shot into the Hells Angels club-house some distance away. He carried two anti-tank rocket launchers with him. During a Hells Angels "Viking Fest" celebrating their anniversary, when about 300 people were in the club-house, and about 100 police officers were outside taking pictures and writing down license plate numbers, the Bandidos prospect fired the first rocket. The rocket flew right through walls of the clubhouse, missing a steel plate by one foot. If it had hit the steel plate and exploded with 3,000-degree heat, many people would have been killed. As it happened, two people were killed. Flying stone fragments from the wall killed a 29-year-old woman in spite of heroic efforts to save her by a police officer who was outside when the rocket hit. Flying shrapnel also killed a Hells Angels prospect. In addition, 18 badly burned others were injured. The Bandidos sniper on the building fled before firing the second rocket.

The brazen nature of the rocket attack in a public space in the afternoon in the middle of Copenhagen created a national outcry and demand for the authorities to take immediate action. Ten days later, the Danish parliament passed a "Rocker Fortresses Law," evicting the bikers from their clubhouses. Citizens joined in the destruction of the clubhouses in their neighborhoods. However, the biker violence continued into 1997 with numerous acts of violence, including murders.

The event that brought the Great Nordic Biker War to an end occurred in Drammen, Norway, a city just east of Oslo. Drammen is a port and river city that is well suited for drug trafficking, a point recognized by both the Hells Angels and Bandidos, who each established chapters in the city. The Oslo Hells Angels president made plans to make his mark in the ongoing battle with the encroaching Bandidos by blowing up the Bandidos chapter in Drammen. On June 4, 1997, six members of a Hells Angels support club packed a stolen minivan with explosives. (As has been pointed out in Chapters 3 and 4, OMGs often use support clubs for the most dirty and dangerous work.) Wearing long-haired wigs and no identifying biker insignias, they drove the vehicle to Drammen and parked it in front of the Bandidos clubhouse. The resulting explosion collapsed the building on sleeping Bandidos members inside, sent debris flying 200 yards away, and knocked the windows out of nearby buildings. The dazed Bandidos staggered outside with all their clothes blown off but uninjured. However, a middle-aged woman and her husband were driving by when the blast went off. The women died instantly, and the man was severely injured.

The public outcry in Denmark, Finland, Norway, and Sweden was immediate and vociferous. Political representatives from all four countries met to discuss banning the motorcycle clubs and pooling their resources to clamp down on them. The bikers sensed they had to do something to calm the situation and protect their illegal crime ventures. The U.S.-based leaders of the two warring biker gangs made the first attempt at peace. According to Sher and Marsden (2006: 253), American representatives of the Hells Angels and the Bandidos met in Colorado and then Seattle to put an end to this costly war and bad publicity. They were trying to establish another Peace Pact. The Danish Hells Angels president and the European Bandidos president beat them to the punch. The war was costing them too much money and it was "bad for business." On September 25, 1997, the two OMC/G leaders, dressed in full colors, shook hands and declared, on public television, that the Great Nordic Biker War was over.

The peace agreement held in the Nordic countries, and both gangs returned to making money through organized crime, with occasional murders of one another over markets and territory. Sher and Marsden (2006) opine that this peace agreement divided up Scandinavia and Europe between the Bandidos and the Hells Angels and lessened the violence between these two powerful criminal organizations. However, the peace agreement had no standing with the Outlaw Motorcycle Gangs such as the Outlaws MC, the Sons of Silence MC, the Warlocks MC, the Mongols MC, the Vagos MC, and other U.S.-based and Australia-based OMGs, not to mention the numerous indigenous OMGs willing to expand into Europe for their piece of the action. Other biker wars between rival Outlaw Motorcycle Gangs in Europe soon occurred. It appears that violence is the only control technique possessed by criminal organizations.

1994–2001: Montreal, Canada, Biker War

This vicious biker war was covered earlier in the book when Canadian Hells Angels leader Maurice "Mom" Boucher was discussed in Chapter 6. The Montreal, Canada, Biker War is the worst organized crime war in history with regard to numbers of dead and injured. The war resulted in 160 murders, 175 attempted murders, 200 wounded, and 15 disappearances (presumed dead). The war between the Rock Machine MC and its organized crime allies and the Canadian Hells Angels was over the domination of the Quebec Province drug trade. Just as in the Great Nordic Biker War, the incidents in public spaces and the presence of innocent victims led to a public outcry and demand for government action. Some called it a "moral panic" based on sensationalized media attention, but one could also view the public outrage as a rational response to such public violence. A civil society cannot tolerate such senseless violence.

1997: Australian Biker Wars

Six people were wounded when warring members of the Bandidos and the Australian Odin's Warriors MC fought it out in the city of Mackay, Australia. Two Australian MC members outside a nightclub in Sydney, Australia, murdered three Bandidos MC members, including the Australian national president and the national sergeant at arms.

1997: Avengers MC Declares War on Iron Coffins MC and the Forbidden Wheels MC

The president of the Avengers MC, which was founded in Michigan in 1997, declared war on the Iron Coffins MC and the Forbidden Wheels MC and directed Avengers to kill members of the rival clubs and take their "cuts." The action ignited a war that resulted in several killed and injured.

1998: Outcasts MC–Hells Angels MC Biker War

The indigenous Outcasts MC were providing security for an Annual Rockers Reunion near the Battersea Arts Centre in the south of London when the Hells Angels decided to send a message to the Outcasts, their traditional rival in the United Kingdom (Sher and Marsden, 2006). Hells

Angels from all over England surrounded the event site. Most of the Outcasts were already in the center, but one arrived late and alone. The Angels dragged that man off his bike and began attacking him with baseball bats, machetes, iron bars, knives, and axes. They hacked him to death. Another Outcasts member arrived and tried to help his fellow biker. He was stabbed to death. The murders took place literally on the steps of the local police station, but the attackers did not seem to be concerned about police presence.

2002: Hells Angels MC and Mongols MC Battle in Laughlin, Nevada, Casino

Known as the River Run Riot, a battle took place on April 27, 2002, inside Harrah's Casino in Laughlin, Nevada, during the 20th Annual River Run Motorcycle Rally. The River Run Rally is the largest and oldest motorcycle rally in the western United States. Although Laughlin is 100 miles from Las Vegas, it is policed by a contractual agreement with the Las Vegas Metropolitan Police Department. Because of the deep hatred between the HAMC and the Mongols, the police were expecting trouble, but not a full-scale confrontation inside a public place like a casino. There had never been any extreme violence at a River Run Rally in the past. To prevent violent encounters, the Hells Angels in attendance stayed at the Flamingo Hotel and Casino, and the Mongols stayed at Harrah's Hotel and Casino some distance away. At approximately 2:00 AM, as many as 35 HAMC members, by some estimates, decided to ride to Harrah's and confront the Mongols. There were several incidents that could have motivated their decision: The Mongols had harassed a Hells Angels member selling memorabilia, there was an earlier murder of a Hells Angels member, or maybe it was just pure hatred for one another. The Hells Angels entered the casino and proceeded to Rosa's Cantina Bar, where they encountered approximately 40 Mongols (www.onepercentersbikers.com). Mongols president Roger Pinney was called down from his room, and he attempted to ease the tension. As he was talking, a member of the Hells Angels landed a flying kick on a Mongols member, and fighting started on the casino floor, sending casino staff and non-biker guests running for cover. It is commonly understood that a Mongols club member fired the first shot, but then other shots were fired. As the savage altercation took place, security cameras recorded the events. The security tapes were made into law enforcement training videos that this author used numerous times in class presentations.

The fighting led to three killed—two Hells Angels members and one Mongols member—and dozens injured, including 15 taken to the emergency room. Six Mongols members were charged and convicted of various crimes, ranging from voluntary manslaughter to attempt to commit battery, and they were sentenced to punishment ranging from probation to five years in prison. Seven Hells Angels members were charged and convicted of committing Violent Crime in Aid of Racketeering (VICAR) and were given sentences ranging from two years to 54 months in prison. An interesting aside to this riot occurred when Harrah's in Laughlin sent letters to previous guests inviting them to come back for a visit to their "now safe" property.

2002: Biker Battle between Hells Angels MC and Pagans MC at the Hellraiser Ball

The deadly fight between the Long Island, New York, Hells Angels chapter and Pagans MC members from all over the Northeast follows a particularly disturbing pattern of outlaw biker violence here and overseas—that is, violence that takes place in a public setting with no regard for the safety of others. The law enforcement authorities anticipated there might be violence of some sort between the competing outlaw biker gangs over contested territory, but few expected violence in a public setting that put civilians—men, women, and children—in danger of death and injury. This dangerous outlaw biker violence pattern is becoming increasingly common since the 1990s, as evidenced in the United States, Australia, Canada, and Europe.

The Long Island HAMC chapter sponsored the Hellraiser Ball in 2002. The location of the event was galling to the Pagans MC because Long Island, New York, was considered Pagans territory until the Hells Angels "muscled" their way in after the Pagans' ranks had been decimated by federal and state law enforcement—and some Pagans members had "patched over" to the expanding Hells Angels. Ready for trouble, law enforcement authorities had both uniform and plainclothes officers inside and outside the event location, and had the front entrance under surveillance (Lueck, February 24, 2002).

There was a motorcycle and tattoo exposition located in the Vanderbilt, a concert hall in Plainview, New York, an area the Pagans considered their territory. Sonny Barger and Chuck Zito, media celebrities and HAMC leaders, were in attendance, enflaming the Pagans' feelings of disrespect. According to court testimony, the Pagans national governing board known as the "Mother Chapter" sanctioned the attack. The war was on.

The depleted Long Island Pagans were unable to wage war, so 70 or 80 Pagans (many from Maryland and Pennsylvania), some wearing bulletproof vests, loaded into vans and convoyed to Long Island. When they arrived at the concert hall, the Pagans, armed with baseball bats, clubs, and guns, rushed the entrance. Luckily, the size of the door only allowed a few to enter at the same time. Those who did enter the concert hall, which was filled with 1,000 men, women, and children, began turning over tables, shooting at Hells Angels, and creating a panic among the terrified civilians. After the shooting ended and the police gained control, the police stopped 13 vans fleeing the scene and found nine Pagans who had been shot, including one who had died of knife wounds and gunshots. The police shut down the Long Island Expressway to prevent any vans or cars with bikers in them to flee. More than 70 Pagans MC members were charged and convicted of assault charges. The Hells Angels member who killed the Pagans member was acquitted of murder charges; he claimed self-defense.

2008: Hells Angels MC and Outlaws MC Battle in Birmingham International Airport, England

According to Judge Patrick Thomas QC, sitting at Birmingham Crown Court, the outlaw biker battle in the Birmingham airport "was an appalling case of public disorder in the presence of and to the terror of probably hundreds of people" (www.birminghammail.co.uk). The judge's words barely capture the surreal event that occurred in Birmingham International Airport on January 20, 2008, as up to 30 outlaw bikers fought with each other with "knuckle busters" (brass knuckles), hammers, and a meat cleaver (Dolan, April 21, 2009; www.dailymail.co.uk). Happenstance brought the two rival gangs (Hells Angels and Outlaws) together in the airport. Members of both gangs were on an airplane flying back from Alicante, Spain, when they spotted each other. Each group called ahead and summoned other members to meet the incoming flight. Up to 30 bikers showed up at the airport and began fighting in the passage joining the two airport terminals, close to where passengers emerge after clearing customs. The violence sent frightened civilians scrambling for safety. Most of the chaos and violence was captured on the airport's closed-circuit television (CCTV). The CCTV footage was shown to the jury at trial.

Four Outlaws MC members and four Hells Angels MC members were tried and convicted of rioting charges. Seven of the eight defendants convicted were sentenced to six years in prison. The eighth defendant, a Hells Angels member, fled to South Africa with what has been described as a "substantial" amount of money. The HAMC has chapters in South Africa.

2009: HAMC and Comanchero MC Battle in Sydney Airport

The enemies of the Comanchero MC are primarily the Bandidos and the Hells Angels MCs. The Bandidos are adversaries because of the split that occurred before the Milperra Massacre (mentioned earlier in this chapter). The HAMC are the enemies of most OMC/Gs because of their elitist attitude and expansion practices. The Comanchero view them as an interloper into Australia and as a competitor in the criminal markets "down under" and in Europe as the Comanchero MC expands there. The Comanchero MC established a chapter in Bosnia and Herzegovina in 2004 and have since established chapters in Spain and Russia as well. Therefore, it is not surprising to outlaw biker followers and experts that a chance meeting between these hated rivals would turn deadly, even in a public setting like an international airport.

Nathan Rees, Premier of New South Wales, said, "I was sickened by this brazen attack. Violence of this nature, particularly in front of families and children, is nothing short of disgusting" (Meikle, March 22, 2009). He was referring to the brawl that occurred in the Sydney domestic airport between the rival Outlaw Motorcycle Gangs the Australian Comanchero MC and the Australian chapter of the U.S.-based Hells Angels MC on March 22, 2009. The deadly brawl occurred when representatives from both gangs found themselves on the same flight to Sydney from Melbourne. The rival groups became agitated and began sending text messages to gang members on the ground (Callinan, March 29, 2009). Allegedly, the leaders of the groups had been to Melbourne for a peace summit to tone down the violence between Australia's biker gangs because they feared a government crackdown that would be bad for business. What happened in the airport did lead to a government crackdown.

The battle between the two groups began immediately when they landed, as those who were on the plane headed to the check-in area. At one point, the fighting bikers knocked over a baby in a stroller. When the bikers reached the secure check-in area, their summoned associates joined them. The bikers grabbed bollards (steel posts used to mark passenger lines) and began bashing one another. A 29-year-old brother of one of the Hells Angels members was knocked to the ground, and the National President of the Comanchero, Mahmoud "Mick" Hawi, crushed the man's skull with a bollard. The victim was stomped on the head on the floor. As soon as the bikers saw the blood coming from the man's head, the 15-minute fight was over, and they quickly exited the airport, with some grabbing taxis to flee.

Hawi was tried and found guilty of the murder and sentenced to a non-parole period of 21 years and a maximum of 28 years. Five other Comanchero members were tried and found guilty of manslaughter. Six members and associates were found guilty of charges ranging from riot to affray and assault. The two gangs left the court and returned to their normal state of hatred and tension.

2015: Waco, Texas, Biker Massacre

The deadliest incident of outlaw biker violence in United States history took place in Waco, Texas, on May 17, 2015. This event is discussed in detail in Chapter 8.

See Table 7.1.

All of the events from Altamont to Waco, and in between, show the expansion of biker violence into public places, putting innocents at risk and gleaning greater attention from law enforcement and the public.

TABLE 7.1 Typology of Planned Aggressive Violence

Year(s)	Participants	Type of Event	Location
1971	HAMC; Breed MC	Biker War	Public Setting, United States
1974	HAMC; Outlaws MC	Biker War	Private Setting, United States
1975	HAMC; Highway 61 MC	Biker War	Private Setting, New Zealand
1977	HAMC; Mongols	Biker War	Public Setting, United States
1980	Galloping Ghosts MC; Bullshit MC	Biker War	Public Setting, Denmark
1983	Road Rats MC; Satans Slaves MC	Biker War	Public Setting, England
1984	Comanchero MC; Bandidos MC	Biker War	Public Setting, Australia
1991	Pagans MC; Fates Assembly MC	Biker War	Public Setting, United States
1994	Outlaws MC; Hells Henchmen MC	Biker War	Public Setting, United States
1994–1997	HAMC; Bandidos MC	Biker War	Public Setting, Denmark, Sweden, Finland, Norway
1994–2001	HAMC; Rock Machine MC	Biker War	Public Setting, Canada
1997	Bandidos MC; Odin's Warriors MC	Biker War	Public Setting, Australia
1997	Avengers MC; Iron Coffins MC; Forbidden Wheels MC	Biker War	Public Setting, United States
1998	Outcasts MC; HAMC	Biker War	Public Setting, United Kingdom
2002	HAMC; Mongols MC	Battle at Casino	Public Setting, United States
2002	HAMC; Pagans MC	Battle at Hellraiser Ball	Public Setting, United States
2008	HAMC; Outlaws MC	Battle in Birmingham Airport	Public Setting, United Kingdom
2009	HAMC; Comanchero MC	Battle in Sydney Airport	Public Setting, Australia
2015	Bandidos MC; Cossacks MC	Battle at Twin Peaks Restaurant	Public Setting, United States

8

THE WACO DEBACLE

Response to a Moral Panic

Introduction

The deadliest incident of outlaw biker violence in United States history took place in Waco, Texas, on May 17, 2015, creating the most recent *moral panic* involving outlaw bikers, as of this writing. This public violence was the trigger event for a media blitz that created a sensationalized national and international debate on outlaw biker violence and law enforcement's reaction before, during, and after the carnage. This debate continues and likely will for years. Outlaw bikers acting as "criminal street gang members" writ large were demonized and blamed for the deaths and injuries, even though the available evidence demonstrated that the pejorative label was false and law enforcement officers killed some people. As events of that day unfolded, law enforcement authorities exhibiting knee-jerk reactions to public fears ran roughshod over the civil liberties of those on the scene. The politicians and law enforcement officials compounded their errors in an attempt to cover up their failures. Law enforcement authorities could have prevented what was a predictable violent encounter between motorcycle clubs. The combatants, the Bandidos MC and the Cossacks MC, had declared war on each other; the police knew it but failed to act.

There are credible allegations of police officers firing indiscriminately into the crowd of men and women coming to a "Sunday Funday" meeting of the Region Texas Confederation of Clubs and Independents. Previously placed police snipers with automatic rifles shot into the crowd. How many they killed or injured is not known definitely, and the authorities have stonewalled all inquiries. Mass arrests of men and women for being members of a "criminal street gang," as defined by Texas statute, and engaging in acts to support organized criminal behavior were made by stunned and excited police officers and an out-of-control prosecutor and his staff. It appears local authorities were more interested in punishing the out-of-town interlopers than seeing that justice was done.

The en masse arrests for serious felony offenses (being members of or supporting the criminal activities of a "criminal street gang") were made in spite of both police and prosecutor being aware that such charges were largely without basis. The prosecutor could have easily discovered that there was no basis for the charges. Any reasonably trained police officer knows women are barred from membership in Outlaw Motorcycle Clubs and gangs. In spite of this, four women were arrested and charged with being members of "criminal street gangs" (OMGs in Texas), including a pregnant bank teller.

The Texas Department of Public Safety (TDPS) knows that all motorcycle riders are not organized "criminal street gang" members, and had defined only one Texas motorcycle club, the Bandidos MC, as a "criminal street gang" at the time of the deadly encounter. At the scene and after the massacre, the TDPS added the Cossacks MC to the "criminal street gang" list, an obvious attempt to justify the arrests. United States law enforcement officers must have probable cause or observe the offense to arrest a person for committing an offense. The process used at Waco for making the arrests as well as the criminal complaints required for such a serious felony were of dubious legality.

A Waco detective stood before a Justice of the Peace—a retired state trooper with no legal training—and swore under oath that more than 170 persons who he did not know and never seen "did ... as a member of a criminal street gang, commit or conspire to commit murder, capital murder, or aggravated assault, against the Laws of the State." How could this be true and accurate? His action raises the specter of perjury and calls into question the entire process of arrest and charging at Waco. Following the signing of boilerplate, "fill-in-the-blank" criminal complaints, the same Justice of the Peace set a bond of $1 million for all those arrested, adding new meaning to the term "assembly-line justice." Bail should be based on individual circumstances, and is to be no greater than what a judge thinks is necessary to guarantee appearance in court. Bail should not be used as punishment as it was at Waco. Such an en masse violation of civil rights and liberties has not occurred in the United States since the Civil Rights Era in the 1960s.

As of this writing, none of the arrested has gone to trial, and there is still no definitive information on how many of the dead and injured were the result of biker violence versus police violence. At least 100 civil suits have been filed, including one by four Grim Guardians MC members for $1 billion. This suit compares the Waco incident to another famous moral panic, the Salem, Massachusetts, Witch Hunt. It will be years before the controversy surrounding what has been called the "deadliest outlaw biker encounter" is settled, if ever. However, the pending civil suits point out that in this particular moral panic, the stigmatized "folk devil" group can resist the label and is in a strong position to make the labelers pay for their ill-timed and reckless actions.

Case Study: Massacre at Waco

More than 200 motorcycle riders and others interested in motorcycle rider issues converged on Waco, Texas, to meet at the local Twin Peaks Restaurant, located in a mall known as the Central Texas Market Place, for a Sunday afternoon meeting of the Texas Region One Confederation of Clubs and Independents (Barker, 2016). The Motorcycle Club Confederations, 60 currently in the United States, came into being to ease tension between competing clubs and to support bikers' causes and reduce biker violence. These are all worthy causes, though not always successful, due to dominant OMGs co-opting the Confederations for their objectives.

Among the clubs who would meet that day were the Bandidos MC and their Texas rival, the Cossacks MC. There was bad blood between these two clubs because the Cossacks were displaying (flying) the Texas bottom rocker on their three-piece colors without the Bandidos' permission. The Cossacks were not members of the Confederation because they refused to pay the fee to fly the bottom rocker, which has been alleged, but not verified, to be $100 per chapter per month. A further complaint alleged that the monthly fee each club paid for membership went to the Bandidos, the dominant Texas OMC/G.

Austin was the usual location for Region One meetings, but allegedly this meeting had been moved to Waco because Waco was in the area claimed by the Cossacks, increasing the possibility of patch and territory dispute. The Texas motorcycle community was aware this move inflamed the already angry Cossacks. The Cossacks made plans to attend as a group in protest. A Cossacks Nomad chapter member sent an email telling all Cossacks that attendance at the meeting was mandatory (Davis, 2015a). Police agencies knew of this change, as well as the Bandidos' desire to "poke a stick in a hornet's nest" long before the May 2015 event (Davis, 2015a). The entire Texas motorcycle community and the Texas law enforcement community knew the meeting in a public setting was a recipe for disaster. Yet, the law enforcement community did not warn the Confederation of Clubs and Independents or the restaurant, or forewarn the public who might be out in the areas of restaurants and shops on a Sunday afternoon. Instead, they made plans to record and respond to the violence and arrest the survivors.

The TDPS warned the state's law enforcement agencies on May 1, 2015, that the Bandidos had declared war on the Cossacks (AP, May, 19, 2015). The TDPS bulletin warned that violence had increased between the Bandidos and Cossacks because the Cossacks were wearing the Texas bottom rocker. It outlined previous violent altercations and the Bandidos war declaration. The Waco police, expecting trouble, positioned a pole camera (which provides surveillance of subjects around corners and barriers) in front of the patio at 7:00 AM on the day of the massacre. It seemed they intended to record the violence, not stop it. Twenty-two police officers, including snipers with automatic rifles, were on the scene, but they took no preventive action.

Approximately 70 of the uninvited Cossacks and their supporters arrived early—at about 10:45 AM for the 1:00 PM meeting. The Cossacks and their supporters used all the parking places directly in front of the restaurant and then settled into all the seats and tables on the patio. The patio was previously reserved for the Bandidos and the other Confederation members. These moves were a red flag that there would be a confrontation, yet the police waited. Police reports indicate police officers saw Cossacks members and supporters walking around the patio, appearing to adjust weapons under their vests and some with handguns and flat-blade knives (Davis, 2015a). In addition, it is alleged by a reliable unnamed source that the police had two to four undercover officers embedded with the Cossacks and present when the shootout was planned and started. A police investigator is quoted as saying, "We thought there was potential for possible fights, but nothing like what took place. In my mind I expected some tension, some arguing, pushing and shoving, fights. I didn't expect that" (*The Aging Rebel*, March 22, 2016). In the face of this naiveté, all hell broke loose, and 60 shots were fired in 109 seconds (Davis, 2015a).

All naiveté ended when the first small group, about a dozen Dallas Bandidos MC members, of the estimated 100 Bandidos, showed up and confronted the Cossacks and their supporters on the patio. Who or what started the deadly shootout is still in dispute. Videotapes show the fighting starting on the patio and then moved into the restaurant and the parking lot. A former Bandidos leader told this author that a "methed up" Dallas Bandidos member shot the first Cossacks member. What's known for sure is that whoever fired the first shot set off a chaotic scene, with bikers fighting each other with a variety of weapons, the warring bikers shooting at each other, and the police snipers shooting into the warring groups.

When the shooting ended, nine bikers were dead—seven Cossacks members, one Bandidos member, and one unaffiliated biker—and 18 wounded. There is no official information on the number wounded by the police (Barker, 2016), but Davis (2015a) alleges that at least four were wounded as a result of police fire. Autopsy results indicate that four bikers were killed by police officers.

At first, all the motorcycle members on the scene were taken to the Waco Convention Center for interviews. At the Conventions Center, Waco Police Department detectives, Texas Rangers, and TDPS special agents interviewed the detained 177 males and females from different and diverse motorcycle clubs. Those detained were told they were witnesses. Sometime in the evening, the decision was made by the prosecutor and the police chief to stop the interviews and arrest all 177 detainees who were wearing "a patch, clothing, or insignia, which indicated support for the Bandidos or Cossacks." This was clearly overreach and guilt by association (Barker, 2016). Those arrested came from multiple chapters of 26 motorcycle clubs, including conventional, social organization, clubs, Outlaw Motorcycle Clubs, as well as a Texas-declared "criminal street gang," the Bandidos.

As noted earlier, during the meeting of law enforcement officials, the Cossacks were also declared "a criminal street gang" by the TDPS (Davis, 2015a), whereas up until then, only the Bandidos MC had been so designated. The cover-up began. The mass arrests and violations of civil rights and liberties had to be justified. No one would be charged with murder. Instead, they would be charged with engaging in organized crime. The capital murder charges would be a separate investigation. This move appears to be a questionable legal maneuver to justify the mass arrests.

As alluded to earlier in this chapter, a Waco police detective who knew nothing about those arrested except their names was presented with photocopies of arrest warrants and signed them as the names were filled in (Barker, 2016). Those arrested were charged with engaging in organized crime due to being members or supporting the criminal activities of a "criminal street gang" as defined by Texas criminal law. Among those arrested were four females (barred from membership in Outlaw Motorcycle Clubs) and several blacks (barred from membership in the Bandidos), including a retired black San Antonio Police Department detective (barred from membership in most OMCs, including the Bandidos). The remaining arrestees included individuals who were not members of Outlaw Motorcycle Clubs or any other defined "criminal street gangs." For example: the president of a club called the Grim Guardians MC, which focuses on caring for disadvantaged and abused children (one of the members arrested was an engineer with the Austin Department of Public Works with degrees from Baylor University and Oklahoma Baptist University); three members of the Vice Grips MC, a conventional motorcycle club whose members restore and ride vintage motorcycle; five members of the In Country Vets MC, a conventional motorcycle club; the aforementioned pregnant bank teller and her husband, an electrician, who are both members of a seven-person family-friendly conventional motorcycle club; another husband-and-wife couple who were members of the Los Pirados, a family-friendly conventional riding club. These innocent persons were only guilty of being in the wrong place at the wrong time (Barker, 2016).

Furthermore, the videos and surveillance cameras reveal that the majority of those inside and outside of the Twin Peaks Restaurant were not involved in the fighting; they were scrambling to find a safe place to hide. The local law enforcement officers, the Texas Rangers, the special agents from the TDPS, and the county prosecutor all knew this, but the information was ignored as the police made the mass arrests, violating their civil liberties.

With the million-dollar bail set, the Justice of the Peace required a nonrefundable cash deposit of $100,000, a sum few could raise. Making it clear that the high bail was punishment for the non-local bikers who had come to his town and wreaked havoc, the Justice of the Peace said, "I think it is important to send a message. We had nine people killed in our community. These people just came in, and most of them were from out of town. Very few of them were from our town" (*The Aging Rebel*, March 22, 2016). A complaint to the State Commission on Judicial Conduct saying the justice's conduct, "while not necessarily appropriate," does not rise to "the level of sanctionable [sic] misconduct" was dismissed (*Waco Tribune-Herald*, February 24, 2016). This ruling set off a stream of outrage from the Texas Criminal Defense Lawyers Association, saying the extreme bonds took weeks to be reduced, causing many to lose their jobs. Furthermore, the delay in getting proper bonds set with "cut-and-paste" arrest warrants was a breakdown in our system of justice (Barker, 2016).

The full effect on those arrested is only now becoming public knowledge, as the civil suits continue to be filed. However, the available evidence supports the disastrous effects on the reputations, employment, and social standing of those who were arrested—people guilty only of being in the wrong place at the wrong time. Those arrested and finally granted bail were subject to humiliating conditions—wearing ankle bracelets, subject to restricted travel conditions and curfews, and prohibited from returning to McLennan County except for court appearances. Many of the arrested suffered collateral consequences. The retired San Antonio police detective with 32 years of service lost his job as a school bus driver because of the felony arrest and underwent a long period in jail waiting for his bail to be lowered. A landscaper fighting a custody battle was faced with an ex-wife using his arrest as her reason to gain full custody. A United Airlines pilot lost his job (Barker, 2016). The International President of the Blue Knights MC, a motorcycle club of 20,000 members including active and retired law enforcement officers, is quoted as saying after the Waco massacre, "Not all the clubs there in attendance were bad guys, so to say. Wrong place, wrong time" (Chasnoff, May 20, 2015).

Conclusion

The legacy of violence in the outlaw biker world has guided the discussion in this book. Outlaw biker violence is endemic and a part of the culture and lifestyle of those who live and travel in their milieu. This has been true since the founding of Outlaw Motorcycle Clubs in the United States in the 1950s and was exacerbated by the movement of many OMCs into organized crime, especially drug trafficking, and evolution into OMGs in the 1960s. The U.S.-based OMGs spread their violence into Australia, Canada, and Europe and now are moving into Asia and the rest of the world. The violence occurs between and among bikers and those they encounter in their social world. There are some "bad men" in the biker world. However, the most disturbing and dangerous violence is that which takes place in public settings, putting innocent persons at risk of death and injury and triggering moral panics such as occurred at Waco, Texas. When government officials and their political agents fashion and execute their reactions to outlaw biker violence based on the resulting moral panic, disastrous consequences can follow their knee-jerk or grandstanding actions.

The deadly encounter in Waco between motorcycle clubs and heavily armed and forewarned police officers on May 17, 2015, is surrounded by controversy that rages on today. It is still not known who bears the major responsibility for what occurred and its aftermath—the law enforcement authorities or the "outlaw" bikers. The mass arrests supported by misclassifying persons as belonging to or supporting "criminal street gangs" caused severe social consequences to innocent persons and resulted in numerous civil rights and liberties violations. The police on the scene could have and should have prevented the violence that occurred.

The lessons learned from the massacre at Waco in May 2015 are: (1) the outlaw biker world is dangerous and violent, and biker violence is most dangerous in public settings; (2) law enforcement authorities must recognize the difference between different types of motorcycle clubs and make decisions made on these distinctions; and (3) the sensationalized media reacting to the triggering events raises public fear—a moral panic—leading to grandstanding by politicians and impulsive reactions that can result in human and civil rights violations. The "folk devil" victims—innocent profiled motorcycle riders wrongly stigmatized—may well make the law enforcement authorities and their government entities pay for their actions.

BIBLIOGRAPHY

Alain, M. (1965). The rise and fall of motorcycle gangs in Quebec. *Federal Probation* 59: 54–57.

Albanese, J. (2012). Deciphering the linkages between organized crime and transnational crime. *Journal of International Affairs* 66(1): 1–16.

Albrecht, L. (July 1, 2009). After weekend fight, Los Banos beefs up security for biker rally: Anti-violence gathering gets ugly when prayer turns to fisticuffs. *McClatchy-Business News*.

Amoruso, D. (November 1, 2011). Biker news: Murder, arrests, one break up & a ban. *Gangsters Inc.* http://gangstersinc.ning.com.

Amoruso, D. (March 20, 2014). Bandidos plant flag in Netherlands, Hells Angels unhappy. *Gangsters Inc.* http://gangstersinc.ning.com.

Amoruso, D. (October 11, 2014). Outlaw bikers join fight against ISIS in Iraq. *Gangsters Inc.* http://gangstersinc.ning.com.

Anon. 1 (2002). In the streets & in the papers: Fighting the image battle with outlaw motorcycle gangs. *RCMP Gazette* 64(3).

Anon. 2 (August 17, 2015). Houston lawyer cuts loses in biker pre-trial. Radiolegendary.com.

Anon. 3 (March 17, 2008). Four police officers indicted in connection with Highwaymen Motorcycle Club investigation. http://lawenforcementcorruption.blogspot.com.

Anon. 4 (November 17, 2005). Canada targets biker gangs in crackdown on organized crime. *Jane's Intelligence Review.*

Anon. 5 (February 17, 2017). Belgium Hells Angels sentenced for drug trafficking. *Brussels Times.*

Anon. 6 (April 9, 2011). Biker gang leader sentenced to 20 years. *The Progress.*

Anon. 7 (October, 1999). Retrial granted in Burdette murder case. *Waikato Press.*

Anon. 8 (March 8, 1971). Five die in clash of cycle gangs. *New York Times.*

AP (May 19, 2015). Memo: Violence long simmered between rival Texas biker gangs. *Associated Press.*

AP (September 18, 2015). Waco police bullets hit bikers in May melee. *Associated Press.*

AP (November 21, 2016). County bans employees from being in some biker gangs. *The St. Augustine Record.*

Appleby, T. (June 22, 2006). It's the end of the Bandidos in Canada: Murder charges leave biker gang's membership depleted, police say. *The Globe and Mail.*

Austin, D.M., Gagné, P., and Orend, A. (2010). Commodification and popular imagery of the biker in American culture. *Journal of Popular Culture* 43(5): 942–963.

Ayling, J. (2011a). Criminalizing organizations: Towards deliberative lawmaking. *Law and Society* 33(2): 149–178.

Ayling, J. (2011b). Pre-emptive strike: How Australia is tackling outlaw motorcycle gangs. *American Journal of Criminal Justice* 36: 250–264.

Baird, G. (November 5, 2011). Nelson Blackburn, a founding member of the Cleveland Hells Angels chapter, dies. *The Plain Dealer*.

Ball, K.R. (2011). *Terry the Tramp: The Life and Dangerous Times of a One Percenter*. Minneapolis, MN: Ball.

Ballard, L.M. (1977). "These youngsters change all these traditions": A perspective on "outlaw" motorcycle clubs in Ireland. *Ulster Folklore*.

Bandler, J. (August 23, 2002). Actor picks going to jail over therapy. *Journal News*.

Barger, R. Zimmerman, K., and Zimmerman, K. (2000). *Hell's Angels: The Life and Times of Sonny Barger and the Hell's Angels Motorcycle Club*. New York: William Morrow.

Barker, T. (2007). *Biker Gangs and Organized Crime*. Newark, NJ: LexisNexis Matthew Bender (Anderson Publishing).

Barker, T. (2014). *Outlaw Motorcycle Gangs as Organized Crime Groups*. New York: Springer Briefs in Criminology.

Barker, T. (2015a). *Biker Gangs and Transnational Organized Crime*. Waltham, MA: Elsevier (Anderson Publishing). Now published by Routledge.

Barker, T. (2015b). *North American Criminal Gangs: Mexico, United States, and Canada*. Durham, NC: Carolina Academic Press.

Barker, T. (2016). Massacre at Six-Shooter Junction (Waco, Texas): Police overreaction to a new folk devil. Presented at the Annual Meeting of the American Society of Criminology. New Orleans, LA, November 16–19, 2016.

Barker, T., and Human, K.M. (2009). Crimes of the big four motorcycle gangs. *Journal of Criminal Justice* 37(2): 174–179.

Barnhardt, L. (January 6, 2004). Motorcycle gang rivalry likely motive for shooting: Two men injured at club as turf war intensifies. *The Sun*.

Barrows, J., and Huff, C.R. (2009). Gangs and public policy: Constructing and deconstructing gang databases. *Criminology and Public Policy* 8(4): 675–703.

Barstow, D. (February 25, 1996). The two Crazy Joes. *St. Petersburg Times*.

Becker, H.S. (1963). *Outsiders: Studies in the Sociology of Deviance*. New York: The Free Press.

Beckett, M. (September 18, 2003). Car-bomb killing in suburbia rekindles Denmark's bitter biker violence. *The Independent*.

Blokland, A., Soudijn, M., and van der Leest, W. (2017). Outlaw bikers in the Netherlands: Clubs, social criminal organizations, or gangs? In A. Bain and M. Lauchs (eds.), *Understanding the Outlaw Motorcycle Gangs: International Perspectives*. Durham, NC: Carolina Academic Press.

Bolan, K. (July 25, 2008). Is missing Angel dead? He welcomed a police informer into the gang. Nine members went to jail. Now he has disappeared. *The Vancouver Sun*.

Bolan, K. (August 13, 2010). Gang's former debt collector had no shortage of enemies, police say; The Hells Angels turfed Juel Stanton. He was shot dead Thursday, a brutal end to a life of crime. *The Vancouver Sun*.

Bolan, K. (March 16, 2007). Debt paid with a finger: Biker enforcer maintains order with murder, mutilations. *The Vancouver Sun*.

Bowe, B. (1994). *Born to be Wild*. New York: Warner Books.

Brumley, J. (May 29, 2015). Waco shoot-out distorts their experience with bikers, say Baptist. BaptistNews.com.

Burnstein, S. (2016). *Biker Gangs in the Motor City: A History of Riding Rough*. http://gangsterreport.com.

Butcher, S. (November 14, 2014). Teen bashed for "having temerity" to say he was a member of Hells Angels. *The Age*. Theage.com.au.

Callinan, R. (March 29, 2009). Outbreak of biker violence leaves Australia on edge. *Time*.

Carlson, L. (2011). Bail schedules: A violation of judicial discretion? *Criminal Justice* 26(1): 13–14.

Carroll, J. (October 11, 2016). Twin Peaks biker killed in crash during police chase. www.kwtx.com.

Cash, A. (2012). First they came for the bikies: A look into South Australia's anti-bikie legislation. *Perspective* 6: 17–32.

CBS Dallas-Fort Worth (May 18, 2016). Timeline of events: May 17, 2015 Twin Peaks biker shootout. www.wacotrib.com/news.

Chachere, V. (March 29, 2001). Defense takes on government's star witness against Outlaws gang. Jacksonville.com/apnews.

Chambers v. *State*. 508 S.W. 2nd 348 (1974).

Chasnoff, B. (May 20, 2015). Not all motorcyclists are "bad guys." *San Antonio Express*.

Cherry, P. (April 16, 2009). Full patch-member turned. Sparked raids. Told police how Quebec Hells Angels okayed biker war in 1994 vote. *Montreal Gazette*.

Cherry, P. (March 16, 2017). Former Montreal cop who sold information to Hells Angel is denied full parole. *Montreal Gazette*.

Christie, G. (2016). *Exile on Front Street: My Life as a Hells Angels and Beyond*. New York: Thomas Dunne Books.

Clearly, T. (May 19, 2015). What biker gangs were involved in the Waco, Texas shootout. Heavy.com.

Cohen, S. (1972). *Folk Devils and Moral Panics: The Creation of the Mods and Rockers*. Oxford, UK: Martin Robertson.

Cohen, S. (2011). *Folk Devils and Moral Panics*. London: Routledge.

Colarossi, A. (February 11, 2011). Jury finds Warlocks member guilty of murder. *Orlando Sentinel*.

Contreras, G. (May 28, 2015). Waco gunfight cases jam local courts. *Houston Chronicle*.

Cooper, L., and Bowden, M. (2006). Working with women associated with bikie gangs: Practical dilemmas. *Australian Social Work* 59(3): 301–313.

Crime.co.nz (n.d.). Malcolm Rewa (Auckland serial rapist). www.crime.co.nz/c-files.aspx?ID=27066.

D'Cruz, N. (November 7, 2014). M'sian Police Help Smash International Crime. *Bernama: Malaysian National New Agency*.

Danner, T., and Silverman, I. (1986). Characteristics of incarcerated outlaw bikers as compared to nonbiker inmates. *Journal of Crime and Justice* 9: 43–70.

Davis, D.C. (2015a). *The Twin Peaks Ambush: A True Story About the Press, the Police and the Last American Outlaws*. Self-published.

Davis, D.C. (2015b). *Twilight of the Outlaws*. Self-published.

Dirmann, T. (May 2, 2002). Looking for a few bad men; Crime: With longtime rivalries renewed, biker gangs have launched aggressive recruiting drives. Recent violence underscores the trend. *Los Angeles Times*.

Dobyns, J. (2009). *No Angel: My Harrowing Undercover Journey to the Inner Circle of the Hells Angels*. New York: Crow.

Dolan, A. (April 21, 2009). Bikers wielded machete and meat cleaver. *Daily Mail*. dailymail.co.uk.

Dow, A. (October 9, 2014). Hells Angels boss Peter "Skitzo" Hewat arrested, Allegedly in possession of erectile dysfunction pills. *The Sydney Morning Herald*.

Dulaney, W.L. (2005). A brief history of "outlaw" motorcycle clubs. *International Journal of Motorcycle Studies* 1 (November).

Ekman, I. (July 11, 2007). Sweden offers little help to victims of rising biker gang. *International Herald Tribune*.

Europol (2010). The threat of outlaw motorcycle gangs (OMCGs) in South East Europe. *OC-SCAN Policy Brief for Threat Notice 002-2010*. Europol.

Europol (December 21, 2012). Fear of turf war between outlaw motorcycle gangs in Europe. Europol press release.

Europol (July 24, 2013). Major international operation against Hells Angels. Europol press release.

Everett, A. (October 26, 2013). Yves "Apache" Trudeau. *The Dawson English Journal*.

Farberov, S. (September 10, 2014). Court hears how triple murder suspect who has implanted horns and "666" tattoo on his face went to Home Depot to buy saws. *Daily Mail.* dailymail.co.uk

Federal Bureau of Investigation (FBI) (April 23, 2013). Final members of outlaw motorcycle gang sentenced on racketeering conspiracy charges. Press Release. U.S. Attorney's Office.

Fernandez, M., Kovaleski, S.F., and Binder, A. (May 19, 2015). 170 bikers charged in melee with roots in the 60s. *New York Times.*

Ferrara, D. (February 6, 2015). 2 men guilty in 2008 Las Vegas chapel melee. *Las Vegas Review Journal.*

Gettleman, J. (March 1, 2000). Driver who killed biker won't be charged: The D.A. says the man was trying to protect himself from members of a San Fernando motorcycle club when he ran over one of the cyclists. *Los Angeles Times.*

Gilbert, J. (2013). *Patched: The History of Gangs in New Zealand.* Auckland, NZ: Auckland University Press.

Gilbert, J. (2017). The history of outlaw motorcycle clubs in New Zealand. In A. Bain and M. Lauchs (eds.), *Understanding the Outlaw Motorcycle Gangs: International Perspectives.* Durham, NC: Carolina Academic Press.

Goins, D. (September 11, 2015). Authorities seek bullet lodged in Twin Peaks shooting suspect's body. www.wfaa.com.

Goldsworthy, T., and McGillivray, L. (2016). An examination of outlaw motorcycle gangs and their involvement in the illicit drug market and the effectiveness of anti-association legislative responses. *International Journal of Drug Policy* 41: 110–117.

Goode, E., and Ben-Yehuda, N. (1994). *Moral Panics: The Social Consequences of Deviance.* Oxford, UK: Blackwell.

Gray, B. (August 3, 2016). Jailer connected to Twin Peaks case indicted. *KCEN.*

Griffin, M., and Leusner, J. (December 17, 1995). Woman recalls life as "property" of Outlaw enforcer. *The Orlando Sentinel.*

Groom, N. (October 7, 2014). Australian outlaw biker gangs are expanding into south-east Asia, recruiting new members and "tapping into underworld opportunities." *Daily Mail.* dailymail.co.uk.

Hall, J. (2008). *Riding on the Edge: A Motorcycle Outlaw's Tale.* Minneapolis, MN: MBI Publishing Company and Motorbooks.

Harris, M. (1985). *Bikers: Birth of a Modern Day Outlaw.* London: Faber & Faber.

Harris, S. (February 28, 2017). Idaho House OKs bill banning profiling of motorcyclists. *Idaho State Journal.*

Hartford, R. (June 18, 2002). The angels born in hell. *Hartford Courant.*

Hawdon, J., Agnich, L.E., and Ryan, J. (2014). Media framing of a tragedy: A content analysis of print media coverage of the Virginia Tech tragedy. *Traumatology* 20(3): 199–208.

Hayes, B. (2005). *The Original Wild Ones: Tales of the Boozefighters Motorcycle Club.* St. Paul, MN: Motorbooks.

Hayes, B. (2011). *The One Percenter Encyclopedia: The World of Outlaw Motorcycle Clubs From Abyss Ghosts to Zombies Elites.* St. Paul, MN: Motorbooks.

Hayes, B. (2016). *Greatest One-Percenter, Myths, Mysteries & Rumors Revealed.* Minneapolis, MN: Motorbooks.

Hendley, M. (March 30, 2012). Hells Angel Kevin Augustiniak gets 23 years up the river for 2001 slaying of Cynthia Garcia. *Phoenix New Times.*

Herbeck, D. (August 21, 2009). Hamburg officer to admit aiding biker gang: Plea deal will allow detective to retire. *Buffalo News.*

Herbeck, D. (September 9, 2009). Agents target biker gang's Harleys: New charges filed in Chosen Few case. *Buffalo News.*

Herbeck, D. (October 8, 2014). Kingsmen not providing information to police. *Buffalo News.*

Hetherly, M. (August 8, 2016). Kingsmen member pleads guilty in connection with murder trial. http://news.wbfo.org.

Houghton, D. (May 2, 2014). Queensland's outlaw motorcycle gang members are overwhelming criminals with serious convictions. *The Courier Mail.*

Hu, T.H. (May 6, 2001). Bisexual biker hit men helped bust the Hells Angels. *The Globe and Mail*.

Huffadine, L., and Crane, E. (September 25, 2015). Straight into custody for ex-Bandidos bikie enforcer Toby Mitchell after police seize $8 million worth of drugs. *Daily Mail*. dailymail.co.uk

Humphreys, A. (2015). Hells Angels under pressure. http://news.nationalpost.com.

Jauregui, A. (May 21, 2015). Texas turf war spurred Waco biker shootout, says expert. *Huffington Post*.

Jenkins, A. (April 21, 2011). New wash: Motorcycle law dredges up 30-year-old cop killing. *Northwest News Networks*. www.npr.org.

Kalogerakis, G. (October 9, 2002). 12 years in prison and a tongue lashing: Former biker enters guilty plea. Earlier trial is told onetime police witness had also set bombs outside cop stations. *Montreal Gazette*.

Kaplan, T. (October 15, 2016). Hell's Angels member shot at funeral in San Jose. *Mercury News*.

Katz, K. (2011). The enemy within: The outlaw motorcycle gang moral panic. *American Journal of Criminal Justice* 36(3): 231.

Kidd, G. (October 10, 2015). Netherlands, Belgium, Germany cooperate on biker gangs. *NL Times*.

King, J. (December 2, 2011). Hells Angels crony Robert Tutokey gets prison time for helping alleged murderous biker/former stock broker flee country. *Phoenix New Times*.

Klement, C. (2016). Crime prevalence and frequency among Danish outlaw bikers. *Journal of Scandinavian Studies in Criminology and Crime Prevention* 17(2): 132–149.

Koppel, J. (July 3, 2015). Waco biker shooting has long legal aftermath. *The Wall Street Journal*.

Lally, C. (June 22, 2015). Biker gang row may have led to killing: Three arrested over shooting of man (51) outside Limerick biker group clubhouse. *Irish Times*.

Lauchs, M., Bain, A., and Bell, P. (2015). *Outlaw Motorcycle Gangs: A Theoretical Perspective*. New York: Palgrave Macmillan.

Lavigne, Y. (1999). *Hells Angels at War*. Toronto: Harper Collins.

Lejtenyi, P. (October 28, 2016). How the Hells Angels conquered Canada. www.vice.com/en_ca.

Leusner, J., and Griffin, M. (January 8, 1996). Former Outlaw: Spaziano enjoyed killing. *The Orlando Sentinel*.

Livingston, A. (September 18, 2014). Unions, bikies threaten witnesses: police. *AAP*.

Love, D.A. (October 5, 2015). Massive Texas biker gang shooting gets soft coverage, but we shouldn't be surprised. www.ukprogressive.co.uk.

Lueck, T.J. (February 24, 2002). Exposition explodes into a deadly fight between rival bike gangs. *New York Times*.

Lyons, D. (2003). *The Bikeriders*. San Francisco, CA: Chronicle Books.

Macedo, D. (November 24, 2008). Wanted: Randy Mark "Mad" Yager for murder, arson, robbery, and more. Foxnews.com.

Manganis, J. (December 30, 2014). Judge orders Hells Angel held in vicious beating. *Salem News*.

Mann, A. (February 28, 2017). Adelaide man Paul Burgess faces deportation after two months with Comancheros bikie gang. www.abc.net.au.

Maqbool, A. (June 11, 2015). Inside a Texas biker gang funeral. *BBC News*.

Martin, P. (December 2, 1992). Look homeward angel cycle icon Sonny Barger kick-starts life as a free man by violating parole. *Phoenix New Times News*.

McBee, R.D. (2015). *Born to be Wild: The Rise of the American Motorcyclists*. Chapel Hill, NC: University of North Carolina Press.

McNab, D. (2013). *Outlaw Bikers in Australia: The Real Story*. Sydney, Australia: Macmillan.

McPhee, M., and Emery, E. (October 9, 1999). Feds "dismantle" motorcycle gang. Denverpost.com.

Meikle, J. (March 22, 2009). Man bludgeoned to death as biker gangs brawl in Sydney airport. *Guardian*.

Mello, M. (2001). *The Wrong Man*. Minneapolis, MN: University of Minnesota Press.

Mellor, L. (September 30, 2014). Robina shooting: Mark James Graham guilty of shooting of alleged former Bandidos member. *ABC News*.

Millage, K. (June 10, 2005). Bandidos sweep nets dozens. *Bellingham Herald*.

Millage, K. (June 19, 2005). Bikers still in custody. *Bellingham Herald*.

Montgomery, P.L. (March 12, 1971). Some praise won by Hells Angels. *New York Times*.

Morgan, G., Dagistanli, S., and Martin, G. (2010). Global fears, local anxiety: Policing, counterterrorism and moral panic over "bikie gang wars" in New South Wales. *The Australian & New Zealand Journal of Criminology* 43(3): 580–599.

Morselli, C. (2009). Hells Angels in springtime. *Trends in Organized Crime* 12: 145–158.

Morton, J. (1999). Rebels of the road: The biker films. In J. Sergeant and S. Watson (eds.), *Lost Highways: An Illustrated History of Road Movies* (pp. 55–66). London: Creation.

Nelson, L.J. (September 21, 2014). One dead, two injured in shooting on 15 Freeway offramp. *LA Times*.

Nichols, D. (2012). *The One Percenter Code: How to Be an Outlaw in a World Gone Soft*. Minneapolis, MN: Motorbooks.

Penn, N. (October 5, 2015). The untold story of the Texas biker gang shoot-out. *GQ*.

Peritz, I. (March 16, 2002). Attacker shot, killed the wrong man, Quebec police say. *The Globe and Mail*.

Peritz, I. (October 26, 2001). Victim of biker violence buried. *The Globe and Mail*.

Queen, W. (2005). *Under and Alone*. New York: Random House.

Quinn, J.F. (1987). Sex roles and hedonism among members of "outlaw" motorcycle clubs. *Deviant Behavior* 8(1): 47–63.

Quinn, J.F. (2001). Angels, Bandidos, Outlaws, and Pagans: The evolution of organized crime among the Big Four 1% motorcycle clubs. *Deviant Behavior* 22: 379–399.

Quinn, J.F. (2007). Sex and hedonism among one-percenter bikers. In A. Veno (ed.), *The Mammoth Book of Bikers*. New York: Carroll & Graff.

Quinn, J.F., and Forsyth, C.J. (2009). Leathers and Rolexes: The symbolism and values of the motorcycle club. *Deviant Behavior* 30: 235–263.

Quinn, J.F., and Forsyth, C.J. (2011). The tools, tactics, and mentality of outlaw biker wars. *American Journal of Criminal Justice* 36(3): 216–230.

Quinn, J.F., and Koch, D.S. (2003). The nature of criminality within one-percent motorcycle clubs. *Deviant Behavior* 24: 281–305.

RCMP (Royal Canadian Mounted Police) (2012/2013). Making a difference in Manitoba. *Royal Canadian Mounted Police: "D" Division/Year in Review*.

Reynolds, T. (2000). *Wild Ride: How Outlaw Motorcycle Clubs Conquered America*. New York: TV Books.

Richmond, R. (2014). Documents detail Ontario Hells Angels club's criminal records. www.sunnenewsnetwork.com.

Roeder, T. (July 6, 2015). Outlaw Motorcycle groups' efforts to recruit military troops is worrisome, officials say. *Colorado Springs Gazette*.

Rossington, B. (January 7, 2013). Biker gangs bring war to Britain: Cops fear clashes as crews roll into Europe. *The Daily Mirror*.

Roundtree, C. (March 5, 2017). Four Bandidos motorcycle gang members who "murdered rival Hell's Angel with a SNIPER RIFLE" in front of his two sons are arrested 10 years after the assassination. *Daily Mail*.

Salamone, D. (June 11, 1997). It's final: Spaziano must stay in prison. *Orlando Sentinel*.

Salamone, D., and Leusner, J. (May 5, 1996). 21 years later rape case could be ticket to freedom. *Orlando Sentinel*.

Sallah, M.D. (June 3, 2001). Toledo's killer biker turns on his Outlaws "brothers." *Toledo Blade*.

Sanger, D. (2005). *Hell's Witness*. Toronto: Penguin Group.

Schiller, D. (May 27, 2016). Year after Waco shootout, case veiled in secrecy. *Houston Chronicle*.

Schiller, D. (June 15, 2016). Court lifts gag order, clears way for bikers to speak freely about Waco melee. *Houston Chronicle*.

Schmall, E. (May 20, 2015). In Sunday's shootout madness, were "innocent" bikers collateral damage? *KSTX San Antonio*.

Schmall, E. (March 23, 2016). More than 150 bikers facing charges in connection to Waco shootout. *AP*.

Selvin, J. (2016). *Altamont: The Rolling Stones, the Hells Angels, and the Inside Story of Rock's Darkest Day*. New York: HarperCollins.

Shadwick, L. (November 11, 2015). Texas Grand Jury takes just 9 hour to indict 106 Twin Peaks bikers. Breitbart.com/texas.

Shadwick, L. (June 21, 2016). Pair of bikers in Twin Peaks shootout case push to recuse Waco D.A. Breitbart.com/texas.

Shapiro, B. (May 26, 2015). Ferguson activist: Racist media treated Waco bikers better than Ferguson rioters. Breitbart.com/big-journalism.

Sher, J., and Marsden, W. (2006). *Angels of Death: Inside the Biker Gangs' Crime Empire*. New York: Carroll & Graf.

Silvester, J. (March 4, 2013). Bandido boss lives to fight another day. *Victoria News*.

Smith, J. (May 19, 2006). The Hells Angels hit. *The Austin Chronicle*.

Smith, J.B. (May 20, 2015). Friends, family claim some arrested bikers shouldn't be jailed. *Waco Tribune*.

Smith, J.B. (June 6, 2015). Released bikers give clashing accounts of Twin Peaks shootout. *Waco Tribune*.

Spencer, B. (September 26, 2014). Caius Veiovis convicted of first-degree murder, kidnapping, witness intimidation in Berkshire triple murder trial. MassLive.com.

St. Louis Today Staff (January 24, 2012). St. Louis County man sentenced in motorcycle gang slayings. www.stltoday.com.

Stephenson, R. (2004). *Milperra: The Road to Justice*. Sydney: New Holland Publishers.

Stranahan, L. (June 14, 2015). Four weeks later: Waco police narrative unravels. Breitbart.com/texas.

Stuart, D.S. (2007). Riding at the margins: International media and the construction of a generic outlaw biker identity in the South Island of New Zealand, circa 1950–1975 (master's thesis). https://ir.canterbury.ac.nz/handle/10092/953.

The Aging Rebel (February, 22, 2012). Paying Michael Kramer. Agingrebel.com.

The Aging Rebel (May 18, 2015). The Waco police massacre. Agingrebel.com.

The Aging Rebel (July 16, 2015). Horror of the day. Agingrebel.com.

The Aging Rebel (September 5, 2015). Sonny Barger responds. Agingrebel.com.

The Aging Rebel (February 2, 2016). Still no arrests in Denver. Agingrebel.com.

The Aging Rebel (February 19, 2016). The hyper-secret Bandidos case. Agingrebel.com.

The Aging Rebel (February 24, 2016). JP Peterson gets a pass. Agingrebel.com.

The Aging Rebel (March 22, 2016). More Waco indictments expected. Agingrebel.com.

The Aging Rebel (March 24, 2016). Yesterday's Waco indictments. Agingrebel.com.

The Aging Rebel (April 5, 2016). Yager takes plea deal. Agingrebel.com.

The Aging Rebel (February 21, 2017). Waco Day 647. Agingrebel.com.

The Aging Rebel (April 4, 2017). Life, death and honor. Agingrebel.com.

The Aging Rebel (April 7, 2017). Vagos murder twist. Agingrebel.com.

Thompson, H.S. (1966). *Hell's Angels: The Strange and Terrible Saga of the Outlaw Motorcycle Gangs*. New York: Ballantine Books.

Trimble, L. (October 25, 2014). Last of fugitive biker gang leader shakes Baja expat community. https://news.vice.com.

U.S. Department of Justice (May 14, 2009). Members of Highwaymen Motorcycle Club indicted on violent crime, drug, and gun charges. U.S. Attorney's Office, Eastern District of Michigan Press Release.

U.S. Department of Justice (December 21, 2010). Outlaws motorcycle gang members found guilty. Washington, DC: U.S. Department of Justice, Office of Public Affairs Press Release.

U.S. Department of Justice (February 13, 2015). Leader of Salem Hells Angels pleads guilty to federal crimes in connection with brutal assault. U.S. Department of Justice, U.S. Attorney's Office, District of Massachusetts Press Release.

U.S. Department of Justice (February 20, 2015). The national president, vice president, warlord, and three members of the Devils Diciples motorcycle gang convicted of racketeering and drug trafficking charges. Washington, DC: U.S. Department of Justice, Office of Public Affairs Press Release.

U.S. Department of Justice (March 16, 2015). Six leaders and members of Phantom outlaw motorcycle club and Vice Lords street gang convicted of violent racketeering-related crimes. Washington, DC: U.S. Department of Justice, Office of Public Affairs Press Release.

U.S. Department of Justice (May 8, 2015). Outlaw motorcycle gangs (OMGs). www.justice.gov.

U.S. Department of Justice (January 6, 2016). Authorities arrest Bandidos outlaw motorcycle organization leadership. U.S. Department of Justice: U.S. Attorney's Office, Western District of Texas Press Release.

U.S. Department of Justice (March 22, 2016). 16 Kingsmen motorcycle club officers, members indicted in major racketeering operation; National president among those indicted. Washington, DC: U.S. Department of Justice: U.S. Attorney's Office, Western District of New York Press Release.

U.S. Department of Justice (March 16, 2017). Six members and associates of the Hells Angels charged in White Plains federal court with racketeering, narcotics, and money laundering offenses. U.S. Department of Justice: U.S. Attorney's Office, Southern District of New York Press Release.

U.S. Immigration and Customs Enforcement (ICE) (May 6, 2013). Canadian trucker sentenced to 12 years for cross border drug smuggling. Department of Homeland Security Press Release.

UN (United Nations) (September, 2002). *Results of a Pilot Study of Forty Selected Organized Criminal Groups in Sixteen Countries*. United Nations: Office on Drugs and Crime.

UNCICP (United Nations Centre for International Crime Prevention) (2000). Assessing transnational organized crime: Results of a pilot survey of 40 selected organized criminal groups in 16 countries. *Trends in Organized Crime* 6(2): 44–92.

United States v. *Bowman* (2002). No. 01-14305, D.C. Docket No. 97-00333 CR-T-30 U.S. Court of Appeals—Eleventh Circuit, August 20.

United States v. *Eischeid* (2003). No. CR-03-1167-PHX-DGC. United States District Court, D. Arizona, 335 F. Supp. 2d 1033 (2003).

United States v. *Ward Wesley Wright* (2003). 343 F.3d 849 (6th Cir. 2003).

United States v. *Wheels of Soul, et al.* (2011). No. 4:11CR00246CDP (June 9, 2011), U.S. District Court-Eastern Division of Missouri.

Veno, A. (2003). *The Brotherhoods: Inside the Outlaw Motorcycle Clubs*. Crows Nest NSW: Allen & Unwin.

Veno, A. (2009). *The Brotherhoods: Inside the Outlaw Motorcycle Clubs*, 3rd ed. Crows Nest NSW: Allen & Unwin.

Veno, A., and van den Eynde, J. (2007). Moral panic neutralization project: A media-based intervention. *Journal of Community & Applied Social Psychology* 17(6): 490–506.

Vergani, M., and Collins, S. (2015). Radical criminals in the grey area: A comparative study of Mexican religious drug cartels and Australian outlaw motorcycle gangs. *Studies in Conflict & Terrorism* 38: 414–432.

Verges, J., and Martin, J. (November 16, 2008). Verdict here unlikely to stop violence. *Argus Leader*.

von Lampe, K. (2003). Criminally exploitive ties: A network approach to organized crime. In E.C. Viano, J. Magallanes, and L. Bridel (eds.), *Transnational Organized Crime: Myth, Power and Profit*. Durham, NC: Carolina Academic Press.

von Lampe, K. (2008). Organized crime in Europe: Conceptions and realities. *Policing: A Journal of Policy and Practice* 2(1): 7–17.

Waco Tribune-Herald (February 24, 2016). Editorial: State judicial commission wisely balanced the law and hard realities. Wacotrib.com.

Wagner, D. (August 25, 2006). Informer links top Angel to murder plot. *Arizona Republic*.

Ward, J.J. (2010). Outlaw motorcyclists: They're not a contrarian reading of Joseph Losey's *These Are the Damned* (1961) and Sidney Furie's *The Leather Boys* (1964). *The Journal of Popular Culture* 43(2): 381–407.

Welborn, L. (August 30, 2013). Biker-turned-lawyer-killer up for parole. *Orange County Register*.

Whittingham, S. (August 19, 2015). Angels of death: SUN INVESTIGATES: Murder, drug-dealing, debt-collecting, extortion and extreme contract violence. thesun.co.uk.

Winterhalder, E., and De Clercq, W. (2008). *The Assimilation: Rock Machine Becomes Bandidos: Bikers United against the Hells Angels*. Toronto: ECW Press.

Witherspoon, T. (May 29, 2015). Hewitt biker files civil rights lawsuit over Twin Peaks arrest. Wacotrib.com.

Witherspoon, T. (June 2, 2015). Dallas lawyer files complaint against JP Peterson over biker bonds. Wacotrib.com.

Witherspoon, T. (June 20, 2015). Answers and evidence in Twin Peaks shootout delayed by case complexity, police caution. Wacotrib.com.

Wolf, D.B. (1991). *The Rebels: A Brotherhood of Outlaw Bikers*. Toronto: University of Toronto Press.

Yarborough, B. (April 3, 2017). Argument between Vagos members led to San Bernardino double homicide. *The Sun*. www.sbsun.com.

Yates, B. (1999). *Outlaw Machine: Harley-Davidson and the Search for the American Soul*. New York: Broadway Books.

Zito, C., and Layden, J. (2002). *Street Justice*. New York: St. Martin's Press.

INDEX

Page numbers in **bold** denote tables, those in *italics* denote figures.